The American Revolution

A Captivating Guide to the American Revolutionary War and the United States of America's Struggle for Independence from Great Britain

Free Bonus from Captivating History (Available for a Limited time)

Hi History Lovers!

Now you have a chance to join our exclusive history list so you can get your first history ebook for free as well as discounts and a potential to get more history books for free! Simply visit the link below to join.

Captivatinghistory.com/ebook

Also, make sure to follow us on:

Twitter: @Captivhistory

Facebook: Captivating History:@captivatinghistory

Contents

Introduction

The United States has been one of the world's greatest powers for almost a century but began its life as a collection of thirteen colonies in the mighty British Empire. The way in which Americans from the Thirteen Colonies rebelled against British rule and successfully secured independence in war was in many ways miraculous. It marked a turning point in history, not only in terms of the birth of a new state, but because this state was founded on the principles of republicanism, freedoms, and rights, something very distinct from the societies of the old European kingdoms and empires. American independence was by no means inevitable. The tale of the birth of the United States is a story of British colonial mismanagement, of a small and dedicated group of remarkable individuals who found a common interest in defending their livelihoods. It is also a story of Britain's European rivals seeking to exploit British weakness with little eventual gain to show for it. The Thirteen Colonies had been brought closer together by the struggle against the British, but the weakness of the central government threatened the survival of the United States almost from the moment peace was signed with Britain. Although the era of the Founding Fathers may seem remote to most people, they continue to shape contemporary political debate.

This book presents a general outline of the American Revolution, focusing largely on the period between the outbreak of rebellion in 1765 until the ratification of the US Constitution in 1789. In homage to the original thirteen colonies, the book is divided into thirteen chapters. Chapter 1 outlines the context of the Thirteen Colonies as British colonial possessions. Chapters 2-4 deals with American responses to British attempts to raise taxation in the Thirteen Colonies, resulting in a cycle of escalating tensions which finally resulted in the outbreak of military hostilities. Chapter 5 assesses the strengths and weaknesses of the American and British armies at the outbreak of the war, and how these dynamics shifted over the course of the conflict. Chapters 6-10 cover the period of military hostilities from the Declaration of Independence in 1776 to the British surrender at Yorktown in 1781, which would lead to the signing of the Treaty of Paris in 1783. Chapters 11 and 12 cover the uneasy period of peace during which the central government was unable to resolve disputes between individual states, resulting in the adoption of a Constitution which strengthened the powers of central government. Chapter 13 briefly outlines the key debates and themes that would run through American history in the half-century following the adoption of the Constitution.

The United States of America has existed as an independent country for two and a half centuries. In contrast to the Holy Roman Empire, which lasted for one thousand years (800-1806), or the Ottoman Empire which endured for over six hundred (1299-1923), the United States remains relatively young. The United States was conceived as a political experiment and a radical departure from the organizing principles of most European states. It was far from certain that the Union would endure in its early years, and the state once again risked disintegration during the Civil War in the 1860s. In an era where political discourse is becoming increasingly polarized, it is worth reflecting on the circumstances of America's foundation and how states with competing interests and statesmen with competing visions joined together to achieve independence and created a political arena for their new conceptions of government. Some of their compromises, such as those over slavery, were misguided and incompatible with their founding aims, but were made on the basis of political expediency at a time when the American republic was constantly under threat from external enemies, including erstwhile allies. This book seeks to remind readers that the United States was created by a set of founding fathers who had competing visions, but shared a common set of principles dedicated to life, liberty, and the pursuit of happiness.

Chapter 1 – Colonial America

The history of the United States of America begins with European settlement of the New World, or the American continent. Although Viking settlers established a presence in Newfoundland in modern-day Canada, it was not until Christopher Columbus' so-called "Discovery of the Americas" in 1492 when European states began to colonize the Americas. Columbus, serving the Spanish monarchy, paved the path for Spanish colonization of Central America and much of South America. The remaining part—Brazil—was settled by the Portuguese. In the process, the colonizers subjugated the native populations. Through a combination of death by disease and intermarriage with the settlers, the native population declined and was assimilated into the culture of the European colonizers. As the first explorers, Spanish control of the American continent extended as far north as the modern American states of Florida, Texas, and California.

Economic factors served as the primary motivation for colonial activity in the Americas. Each year Spanish galleons laden with gold and silver would sail across the Atlantic to fill the coffers of the king's treasury. In the long run, this would prove to be a mixed blessing, as the import of such large quantities of American gold and silver into Europe devalued the currency. Moreover, these rich treasure ships served as targets for pirates and corsairs. Although in the 16th century the English Royal Navy could not challenge Spain on equal terms, the English sailor Sir Francis Drake began his career looting Spanish ships in the Caribbean and sending the treasure to Queen Elizabeth I's (1558-1603) Exchequer, or treasury. Over the 17th century, Spanish naval supremacy would come under threat of the so-called Maritime Powers—the Netherlands, which won independence from Spain in 1648 after an eight-year struggle, and England, which became Britain after the Act of Union with Scotland in 1707. Taking advantage of declining Spanish naval control over the Atlantic, the British and Dutch established colonies in the Caribbean and in North America, and they were not the only European powers to do so. France would take control of large parts of modern-day United States and Canada. Sweden, Denmark, and even the tiny Duchy of Courland in the Baltic also established colonies in the Caribbean.

British, French, and Dutch settlements in the Americas was also the result of economic motivations, though the source of wealth was of a different nature than that of Spain's colonial possessions. While North America and the Caribbean did not have the rich deposits of precious metals that Spanish possessions in Mexico and Peru enjoyed, the climate was conducive to growing cash crops such as sugar, coffee, and cotton. While these crops were highly lucrative, their cultivation was highly labor-intensive, and the European colonialists lacked the manpower to fully exploit the wealth of the land. As a result of this demand for labor, a triangular trade developed between Europe, Africa, and the Americas, controlled by the Europeans. The Europeans sent manufactured goods to Africa in exchange for slaves, who were transported to the North American colonies to work the land. The harvested crops and raw materials would then be imported into Europe for consumption and further processing. These goods would be used to buy more slaves from Africa, and so the trade continued, operating until the 19th century.

British settlement in North America was largely restricted to the Eastern seaboard, from Massachusetts in the North to Georgia in the South. In addition to its Canadian possessions, British colonists established thirteen colonies over the course of a century between the 1620s and 1733, when the colony of Georgia was founded. British settlement did not extend much farther west due to the Appalachian Mountains which served as a geographical barrier to further movement. The British also came into conflict with native populations who often emerged victorious in small-scale engagements with the outnumbered colonists. They were also forced to compete with European rivals.; in fact, some British colonies were originally founded by rival European powers. The city of New York was founded by Dutch colonists as New Amsterdam before the British seized control in 1664 and renamed the city after the Duke of York. The surrounding Dutch province, New Netherland, was also renamed New York. While the Dutch were easily defeated, the French settled and lay claim to the Louisiana Territory, comprising of Eastern Canada and much of the Mississippi River Basin on the opposite side of the Appalachians. Meanwhile, the Spanish had a foothold in Florida. As a result, British settlement south of the St. Lawrence River was largely confined to the Thirteen Colonies.

Although the British colonists in America were mostly loyal subjects of the British monarch, they did not share a common "American" identity and instead identified with the colonies in which they lived. A series of interrelated geographical, social, and economic factors contributed to the divergence in the cultural development of the Thirteen Colonies. British possessions in North America could be divided into three distinct groups: New England (New Hampshire, Massachusetts Bay, Providence and Rhode Island, Connecticut); the Middle Colonies (New York, New Jersey, Pennsylvania, Delaware); the Southern Colonies (Virginia, Maryland, North Carolina, South Carolina, Georgia). While most economic activity in the colonies was dominated by agriculture, this was especially true of the Southern Colonies. These large territories supported a plantation economy which depended heavily on slave labor. Slave revolts were frequent but small-scale and easily suppressed. In the smaller colonies in New England, the climate and geography were not conducive to cash crops. The economy was geared toward small-scale industrial activities including the manufacture of rum and shipbuilding. The major ports of New York and Boston, Massachusetts became thriving centers of international trade. Slavery existed in the North, but slaves were employed as domestic servants rather than agricultural laborers.

The economic potential of the New World attracted large numbers of immigrants. Thousands of settlers were enticed by the opportunities offered by colonial companies and made the journey across the Atlantic. Although the voyage was perilous and settlers were prone to succumbing to disease, survivors could look forward to prosperous and comfortable lifestyles. Unlike in Europe, where land was expensive and owned by aristocrats, land was cheap and plentiful for the European colonists who arrived in the New World. The lower classes enjoyed better living standards than they had in Europe. Through a combination of natural population growth and immigration, the European population in the Thirteen Colonies increased fivefold between 1650 and 1700 from 55,000 to 265,000. The population would reach one million by 1750. In 1751, the Pennsylvanian botanist John Bartram portrayed the Thirteen Colonies as paradise on earth:

> England already has an uninterrupted line of well-peopled provinces on the coast, successively begun within less than 150 years. Every year they are augmented by an accession of subjects, excited by the desire of living under governments and laws formed on the most excellent model upon earth. In vain do we look for an equal prosperity among the plantations of other European nations.

The waves of immigration into the New World was not only motivated by economic factors, but also by religion. Since the Protestant Reformation in 1517, Europe was embroiled in religious conflict between Catholics and Protestants, which reached a climax with the outbreak of the Thirty Years' War (1618-48). Even within Protestant countries, more radical sects came into conflict with established Anglican and Lutheran churches and suffered prosecution. In 1620, the Pilgrim Fathers sailed from Plymouth in southern England to the New World and established Plymouth Colony in Massachusetts Bay, the first permanent colony in New England and the second British colony after Jamestown, Virginia. The pilgrims were Puritans, a radical Protestant sect which sought to remain separate from the Anglican Church. In 1607, they fled the political and religious turmoil of England and settled in the Netherlands, which was relatively tolerant and open to radical Protestant refugees. The difficulties in learning the Dutch language and in finding employment in the Netherlands caused many to return to England by 1617. They then conceived of a plan to sail across the Atlantic and establish a colony in the New World, allowing them to retain their English identity and live in a society governed by their religious principles.

Due to the legacy of the Pilgrim Fathers, the entire region of New England came to be dominated by Puritans. The other colonies were more diverse in terms of religiosity. The Middle Colonies were especially receptive to foreign immigration. A large Irish population—both Protestant and Catholic—settled in New York. German Lutherans migrated in large numbers to Pennsylvania. Anglicans and Baptists dominated the South. Although British immigrants to the Thirteen Colonies were outnumbered by other nationalities during the 18th century, the existing Anglo-Saxon population naturally increased over the course of the 17th century to the extent that a majority of the European population in North America had British ancestry.

The Thirteen Colonies diverged not only in their religious identities and their economic structures, but also in their political structures. While the French and Spanish monarchies exercised direct rule over their territories in the New World, British colonization of the Americas began as private ventures. The earliest colony, Virginia, was owned by the Virginia Company, which was established to finance the colonization. These colonies were known as charter colonies since they were established by companies which had been granted a royal charter. Most colonies were initially established by charter companies. Since the colonization was privately financed, the ventures came at no cost to the British monarchy. The Crown would grant the colonists a charter establishing the rules of government, but charter colonies effectively ruled themselves. All the colonies operated under English common law, and each colony had a bicameral legislature based on the British Parliament in Westminster. The lower house, or assembly, was chosen by electors—largely male property-owning Christians. The upper house, or council, would be appointed by the governor, usually a royal appointee. The powers of the legislatures depended on the extent to which governors played an active role in political life. At the local level, forms of government differed between the regions. The Northern colonies were more urbanized and town councils were the primary form of local government. The rural Southern Colonies relied on rule at the county level. Both town and county rule co-existed in the Middle Colonies.

Over the course of the 17th century, the British state began to take a greater direct interest in North America. Wars against the Dutch and French in Europe spilled over into the New World. The British armed forces were employed against the Dutch and French in North America and seized control of their territories. The Crown granted these territories to trusted individuals and families who would rule the territory as a representative of the British sovereign. Colonies governed by such individuals were known as proprietary colonies. When New York was seized from the Dutch, King Charles II (1660-

85) granted the colony to younger brother James, Duke of York, to rule as a proprietary colony. When the Duke of York became King James II (1685-88), New York became a royal colony directly ruled by the king. Another major proprietary colony was Pennsylvania, which was granted by King Charles II to William Penn in 1681 in recompense for a debt he owed to Penn's late father, Admiral William Penn. Over the course of the 17th century, many charter companies were deprived of their charters as the British Crown assumed direct rule. These royal colonies were ruled by governors appointed by the British sovereign. Although most of the colonies would fall under direct rule, during the first half of the 18th century, royal governors continued to allow colonial governments a significant degree of autonomy. In an arrangement which came to be called Salutary Neglect, the governors appointed by the British monarch were happy enough to allow the colonists effective self-government so long as they continued to generate tax revenue for the British state through their economic activities.

Chapter 2 – The Seven Years' War and Its Consequences

The British government's policy of Salutary Neglect was a successful formula until the Thirteen Colonies were threatened by war. Although the colonists were keen to take up arms to defend themselves, the government in London was suspicious of colonial attempts to establish a military force independent from London's command. A previous attempt by the New England Colonies to create an alliance to protect against French and Indian threats contributed to the British government's decision to revoke the charters of the colonies. North America was relatively tranquil during the first half of the 18th century, but conflicts in Europe were starting to spread in the New World. The War of Spanish Succession (1701-14) had already seen British and French armies clash in North America. In 1740, Europe was rocked by a political earthquake in the form of King Frederick II of Prussia (1740-86), who would redraw the map of Europe by seizing Silesia from the Austrian Habsburg Empire. The shock to the Habsburgs was so great that they opted for an alliance with France—the Empire's archenemy for over two centuries—in an effort to regain the territories they lost to Prussia.

In 1756, an alliance consisting of Austria, France, and Russia declared war on Frederick in an effort to restrain Frederick's expansionist aims. In Europe, Prussia could only count on Great Britain as an ally. While the British Crown had a presence in continental Europe by virtue of the fact that King George II (1727-60) was also Elector of Hanover, the British and Hanoverian armies were of limited value to Frederick and could not make a major difference in land battles. Britain's strength lay primarily in its formidable navy, which could attack French overseas colonies and distract attention from the European theater. The border between British and French territories in North America was disputed by both sides and this influenced decision-making in London. The ensuing Seven Years' War (1756-63) thus acquired international dimensions. While the European theater may be considered a life-or-death struggle for Frederick the Great's Prussia against three much larger enemies, the Seven Years' War was also part of an Anglo-French struggle for global hegemony encompassing the Americas as well as Asia and Africa.

The North American theater of the Seven Years' War was also known as the French and Indian War. Hostilities began in 1754 as the French and British disputed the border between their respective territories. The French constructed a series of forts along the Ohio River Valley. In May, British colonial militia under the command of 22-year-old Colonel George Washington ambushed a French party on its way to Fort Duquesne, a French fort which occupied a major strategic position at the junction of three rivers. Washington ordered the construction of nearby Fort Necessity as a base. However, he was soon forced to surrender the fort to the French when counterattacked. In June 1754, representatives from eleven colonies met in Albany, New York in an effort to establish a confederation which would provide for mutual protection and allow the colonies to present a united front in diplomatic negotiations with Indian tribes. The plan for a union was developed by Benjamin Franklin, a Pennsylvanian polymath who was heavily involved in Pennsylvanian politics. Franklin encouraged support for his plan by producing a cartoon featuring a snake divided into several parts with the caption "Join or Die." Franklin proposed that the new entity would be ruled by a president appointed by the British Crown. While the Albany Congress passed an amended version of Franklin's plan, it was not ratified by the colonial legislatures nor by the British Crown. The dream of union between the Thirteen Colonies would have to wait.

Hostilities in North America intensified once the French and British became embroiled in the war in Europe. The British government began to send regular army units to America commanded by British officers. Although the British authorities demanded that the colonists provide material support for the war effort, they looked down on the colonial militia, causing considerable resentment among men who considered themselves Englishmen. Meanwhile, reinforcements from the French regular army were also sent to American shores. During the initial stages of the war, the French armies enjoyed several successes. Since the French population in North America was a mere five percent of the British population, they decided to form alliances with Indian tribes to bolster their numbers. In August 1757, a French and Indian force under the command of General Louis-Joseph de Montcalm laid siege to Fort William Henry in New York. The commander of the British garrison negotiated a surrender to the besieging army, but Montcalm's Indian allies, deprived of war trophies, broke the agreement and massacred hundreds of British inhabitants, including women and children. The notorious incident strengthened the resolve of the British army and influenced the decisions of the British military command for the remainder of the war.

Military fortunes turned in Britain's favor after the end of 1757. The British successfully held off further assaults from Montcalm. While British reinforcements and supplies were regularly shipped to North

America from Britain, the British Royal Navy's naval supremacy hindered French attempts to supply Montcalm. In the summer of 1757, the British government was reorganized following earlier defeats. As secretary of state for the Southern Department in the British government, William Pitt took charge of British foreign policy and the war effort. He proposed a new strategy to tie down French armies in Europe by raising a British army for operations in the European continent, while offering Frederick the Great large subsidies to keep large Prussian armies in the field. In the meantime, the Royal Navy would support expeditions to seize French colonies around the world. Already in 1757 British forces achieved success against the French in India. At the Battle of Plassey in June, Robert Clive led the British East India Company's private army to victory over a French ally in the region. Clive's victory established British rule in Bengal and eventually enabled the British Empire—through the East India Company—to control the entirety of the Indian subcontinent.

In North America, Pitt's strategy called for the conquest of Canada. In 1758, a British force commanded by General Jeffrey Amherst successfully captured the fort of Louisbourg on the mouth of the St. Lawrence River. This enabled the British to proceed to Quebec, the capital of New France and a key strategic target for British forces. Pitt appointed General James Wolfe to lead an army to lay siege to Montcalm's forces in Quebec. Wolfe's army, which was outnumbered by the enemy, lay siege to the city in June 1759. The British maintained the siege for three months, but illness began to spread through the British camp and Wolfe opted for decisive measures. On September 13th, he launched a daring assault at the Plains of Abraham overlooking the city. Wolfe took Montcalm by surprise and the momentum of his men was unstoppable. The British won a famous victory in less than an hour, but Wolfe was killed as he led his men on a charge. Montcalm was mortally wounded and died the following day. Wolfe's victory soon led to the British conquest of New France. French efforts to launch an invasion of

Britain failed, and British forces captured Montreal the following year. The war in Europe would last until 1763, but British victory in North America was effectively secured by 1760.

The British may have won the war in North America against the French, but they lost the peace. The war amplified a range of disputes between London and the colonies, and the British government sought to take a more active role in the governance of the Thirteen Colonies. During the 18th century, political power in the United Kingdom gradually transferred from the king (or queen) to Parliament. The British Parliament consisted of an upper house, the House of Lords, and a lower house, the House of Commons. Both chambers sat in opposite wings of the Palace of Westminster. The Lords were unelected landowners who inherited their titles and estates, or were granted them by the king. The Commons was made up of Members of Parliament (MPs) chosen by the electorate—although the vote was limited to a fairly small number of property-owning men. The king would then appoint a government of ministers who could command the support of both Houses of Parliament. The British political system was dominated by two parties, the Tories, who tended to support the king, and the Whigs, who envisaged a greater role for Parliament. However, party affiliations were fluid and governments usually included both Whig and Tory ministers. Since 1721, the British government was led by a prime minister. The first man to assume this role, Robert Walpole (1721-42), proved himself indispensable to King George I (1714-27) in his interactions with Parliament. Walpole remained in this exalted role until 1742 and continues to hold the record for the longest-serving British prime minister.

During the Seven Years' War, the Duke of Newcastle, Thomas Pelham-Holles, served as prime minister (1757-62), although William Pitt effectively shared power as Southern Secretary. Newcastle's Whig government fell in 1762 following the intervention of King George III (1760-1820). The new king believed the Newcastle-Pitt ministry was encroaching on royal privileges and instead championed the cause of the Earl of Bute, who became the first Tory prime minister (1762-63). Although the British were victorious in the Seven Years' War, the conflict was expensive and Britain's national debt doubled as a result. Lord Bute's government believed that the colonies had not contributed enough resources to support the British army in America. Accordingly, the government took steps to establish a greater degree of central control over the colonies. The Westminster government provided for a British regular army of 10,000 men to be stationed in North America to protect colonial interests, which would be paid for by the colonials.

Unsurprisingly, the colonies resisted efforts to be ruled from London and defended their autonomy. The colonials had not been allowed to fight to protect themselves, but were asked to pay for British regular troops. The British army's dismissive attitude toward the colonial militia also led to resentment. During the war, George Washington, the young officer who was involved in the outbreak of hostilities, had been promoted to the rank of brigadier general in the colonial militia. In 1758 he took part in operations which finally led to the conquest of Fort Duquesne, which was replaced by Fort Pitt—now the city of Pittsburgh. Washington hoped to be recognized as an officer in the British regular army, but he was denied the royal commission he dearly sought.

The Seven Years' War had strengthened the bonds between the colonies, despite the failure of the Albany Congress. After seeing off the threat from the French armies, the American colonials recognized the new threat posed by their imperial masters, the British government. Increasing tensions between the two sides became apparent in 1763 following the signing of the Treaty of Paris, which officially ended the Seven Years' War and ceded French territory to Great Britain. Under the terms of the treaty, France ceded its claims east of the Mississippi River to Britain. The population of the existing thirteen British colonies in North America expected to settle in these newly conquered territories. Instead, the colonies once again had cause to feel surrounded and isolated. On

October 7th, 1763, King George issued a royal proclamation which confined colonial settlement east of the Appalachian Mountains. Territories west of this line became part of an Indian reserve. During the Seven Years' War, the British had promised the Indians that they would be able to remain on their lands if they abandoned their support for the French. The British decided to honor these promises, rather than the promise of expansion they made with the colonials. Only the British Crown could decide to move this demarcation line farther to the west. Over the subsequent decade, colonial and British land speculators successfully lobbied the British government to open up territories farther west. However, by this time, the Thirteen Colonies were in open rebellion against the British government.

Chapter 3 – Taxation Without Representation

The Treaty of Paris which ended the Seven Years' War was received poorly in London as well as in the colonies. Lord Bute's leniency toward Britain's foes in the war cost him political popularity and he was deprived of King George's favor. In April 1763, the king dismissed Bute and appointed George Grenville (1763-65) in his stead. Although Grenville identified as a Whig, he had been a minister in Bute's government and he retained most of his predecessor's ministers. Accordingly, he pursued a similar policy with regard to Britain's relationship with its North American colonies. In April 1764 Parliament passed the Sugar Act, which aimed to strengthen enforcement of collection of customs duties on sugar. The new legislation damaged the economy of the New England ports which was heavily dependent on the sugar trade. Trade flows were diverted from New England toward the British West Indies, which was unaffected by the tax. A small number of merchants in New England staged protests against the measure by boycotting British goods, though these acts of resistance were of low intensity and were restricted to New England.

The Sugar Act would raise insufficient revenue to finance British military presence in North America. When he introduced the Sugar Act, Grenville announced that "it may be proper to charge certain stamp duties in the said colonies and plantations." Stamp duties were already in the statute books in the United Kingdom, and proved to be an efficient method for the British Exchequer to collect revenue. All documents could only have legal force if stamped, and anything that did not bear a stamp could be rejected as void. The prospect of a new tax made the colonies anxious, and they sought more information on the proposed measures. When colonial agents met with Grenville in May 1764, they insisted that the taxes should be raised by colonial assemblies rather than the British Parliament. Grenville reassured them that he was willing to consider any measure so long as it raised the required revenue, though he provided little insight into how he intended to implement the tax.

Over the following months, it became clear that Grenville was ignoring the colonials' request and planned to impose a direct tax from Parliament. In February 1765, another group of colonial agents met with Grenville to discuss the proposals. The four-man delegation was composed of Benjamin Franklin of Pennsylvania, Jared Ingersoll and Richard Jackson, both representing Connecticut, and South Carolina's Charles Garth. Both Jackson and Garth were also MPs representing English constituencies. The colonial agents repeated their recommendation that the Americans should be allowed to tax themselves. Jackson argued that if Parliament were given the right to directly tax the colonies, royal governors would no longer need to convene the colonial assemblies to raise taxes. Grenville dismissed these concerns. The colonial agents failed to stop Grenville from introducing the tax, which passed through both Houses of Parliament in February and received royal assent in March 1765. Under the terms of the tax, the British government imposed a tax on all commercially printed material in the colonies. The highest taxes applied to court documents and land grants. Taxes also applied to playing cards and dice, a key aspect of 18th-century entertainment and social life. The tax would be enforced by a stamp distributor, a public official appointed by London.

The Stamp Act soon became the most contested item of legislation in the history of British rule in America. The colonials challenged the legislation, not only due to its economic effects, but on grounds of political principles. The debate over the Stamp Act was centered on two opposing interpretations of the British constitution. Grenville and his ministers were adamant believers in the doctrine of parliamentary sovereignty. Under this principle, the British Parliament in Westminster was the supreme lawmaker of the land, and its right to make laws could not be challenged by any other entity or individual. The colonials, on the other hand, who regarded themselves as subjects of the British Crown and entitled to all the rights enjoyed by the imperial center, believed that they had the right to be taxed only if they consented through representative institutions. As early as 1754, Benjamin Franklin raised this issue when he wrote that "it is supposed an undoubted right of Englishmen not to be taxed but by their own consent given through their representatives." The American colonies were not represented in the British Parliament in Westminster and were instead ruled from London by royal governors. The colonies had their own representative legislative assemblies which were more than capable of raising taxes. Consequently, Franklin and others would argue that taxes could only be levied by colonial assemblies rather than directly by the Parliament in Westminster.

A series of protests spread throughout the Thirteen Colonies under the slogan "No taxation without representation." The scale of the protests was unexpected for both the British government and the American representatives stationed in London. Despite their opposition to the Stamp Act, Benjamin Franklin encouraged a friend to seek appointment as a stamp distributor, and Jared Ingersoll successfully secured for himself the office in Connecticut. The common people refused to use the stamps and ended up burning them instead. Protestors took to the streets and targeted stamp distributors, sometimes even before they disembarked from their ships after the journey from Britain. Their effigies were paraded in the streets and mock executions were staged. In August 1765, a radical organization called the Sons of Liberty was formed in Massachusetts. This group aimed to remove Andrew Oliver, who had been chosen as the stamp distributor for Massachusetts. The Sons of Liberty mobilized the mobs in Boston and encouraged them to target Oliver. He eventually resigned after the rioters burned down his office building. Lieutenant Governor Thomas Hutchinson, a known supporter of the Stamp Act, was also targeted and his house ransacked. Radicals from other colonies soon established their own branches of the Sons of Liberty, using the same methods of intimidation against their stamp distributors. By November, twelve of the thirteen stamp distributors were forced to resign their offices.

The protests and riots in the streets accompanied opposition to the Stamp Act through official political bodies. At the end of May, the Virginia House of Burgesses approved a set of resolutions which stated that Parliament had no authority to tax the colonies. The Virginia Resolves were introduced by a young lawyer named Patrick Henry, who was making his first appearance as a member of the body. In a sense, Henry's position was not revolutionary, since he based his arguments on the basis of rights enjoyed by Englishmen under England's "ancient constitution." Henry's most radical resolve, which was not passed but was printed in newspapers in Rhode Island and Maryland, declared that anyone who defended Parliament's right to tax the colonies would be deemed "an enemy to His Majesty's colony." By the time the Virginia Resolves were passed, most of the colonial legislatures had already dissolved for the summer break. By the time they reconvened in the fall, they followed Virginia's lead. After intense debate, other colonial assemblies passed resolutions denying Parliament the right to tax the colonies. In October, representatives of nine colonies convened the

Stamp Act Congress in New York and issued a similar declaration, and petitioned the king and Parliament to repeal the act.

In London, the scale of the protests against the Stamp Act were eventually recognized, and Parliament felt obliged to reexamine the legislation. They were motivated to do so, not only as a result of violence in the colonies, but due to reports from the British merchant community that their revenues suffered as a consequence of a decline in colonial exports. By the end of 1765, Grenville's ministry had already fallen and was replaced by a ministry led by the Marquis of Rockingham. This new ministry believed that the Stamp Act should be repealed, but could not be certain that the repeal measure would win a parliamentary vote. In a series of powerful speeches in the Commons chamber, William Pitt defended the right of the American colonials to protest and argued that they should be taxed by their own institutions. In response, Grenville, who remained an MP, argued that backing down on the Stamp Act would encourage the rebellion to become a revolution. Eventually a compromise was agreed in Parliament. The government moved a bill to repeal the Stamp Act, arguing that further attempts to enforce the Stamp Act would lead to civil war among the Thirteen Colonies. At the same time, the government introduced the Declaratory Act which affirmed Parliament's right to tax the American colonies "in all cases whatsoever." Both pieces of legislation passed on the same day, March 18th, 1766.

The repeal of the Stamp Act was met with jubilation in the colonies. Representatives of twelve colonial legislatures—with the notable exception of Virginia—passed resolutions to give thanks and profess their loyalty to the king. The initial euphoria was curtailed once the colonials began to consider the implications of the Declaratory Act. Meanwhile, London once again experienced a change in government. Rockingham's ministry was unable to command the support of Parliament. The king turned to William Pitt to form a government, despite the mutual antipathy between the two men. Pitt had already refused the king's approaches on three previous occasions, but finally relented. Aged 57, Pitt retained his reputation as a national hero during the Seven Years' War and pursued an ambitious policy to restore order in the colonies and to unite competing factions in the British Parliament. Pitt's decision to accept the title of Earl of Chatham and enter the House of Lords limited his ability to pursue these plans. Pitt, now referred to by his noble title of Lord Chatham, no longer had the right to sit in the House of Commons, the primary arena for political debate. Thus, proceedings in the Commons were led by Charles Townshend, Chancellor of the Exchequer in Chatham's government. Townshend's power increased after Chatham fell ill in March 1767. He proposed a series of measures including the Revenue Act, which imposed customs duties on a number of goods including lead, glass, paper, and tea. The chancellor believed these duties would be more amenable to the colonies, since they were not levied on internal transactions among the colonies, but on external transactions across the seas with British ships.

The Townshend Acts would provoke another set of riots in North America, though Townshend himself would not live to see the consequences, dying suddenly at the age of 42 in September 1767. Debates over the Townshend Acts were more nuanced than those over the Stamp Act. Many colonials accepted that the customs were legal, but that they were nevertheless unjust and improper. New England merchants were encouraged to refuse to import British goods while the colonies attempted to develop industry in New England to replace them. Massachusetts was the first to organize political resistance to Townshend's measures. In February 1768, Samuel Adams, a brewer and influential public figure in Massachusetts, authored the Massachusetts Circular Letter addressed to the other colonies, advising them to join together in opposition to the Townshend Acts. The measure was passed on the second attempt by the Massachusetts House of Representatives, and the Circular Letter was received enthusiastically by Virginia, which submitted a petition to Parliament to revoke the Townshend Acts. Many colonies also passed nonimportation agreements, despite knowing that it would damage the economic interests of the New England ports. The Circular Letter prompted the British to dissolve the House of Representatives and send British army units to maintain order in the city of Boston. Tensions between civilians and British soldiers reached a climax on March 5th, 1770 when a group of eight British soldiers fired on a mob and killed five people. The eight infantrymen were charged with murder, but most were acquitted after a trial thanks to the efforts of their defense lawyer John Adams, a cousin of Samuel Adams. Adams argued that the soldiers acted out of self-defense. Two of the soldiers were charged with manslaughter but received light punishments.

Despite the acquittal of the British soldiers, the incident became known as the Boston Massacre and strengthened colonial opposition to the British authorities. In fact, on the same day as the Boston Massacre, the Revenue Act, the most insidious of the Townshend Acts, was partially repealed by Parliament. The repeal was initiated by Lord North, a Tory who became Prime Minister in January 1770 and would remain in office for another twelve years. While some parliamentarians supported a full repeal, North wished to retain the duties on the import of tea, which was formalized with the Tea Act of 1773. The Tea Act had partially been passed in order to increase the revenues of the East India Company, which was exempt from the taxation applied to colonial merchants. Although these parliamentary measures lessened the burden of taxation on the colonies, the colonials interpreted the Tea Act as yet another attempt by Parliament to assert its right to tax them. Sons of Liberty groups in Pennsylvania and New York were the first to resist the Tea Act and did so by preventing the import of tea into their harbors. In Boston, Samuel Adams was equally keen to ensure that merchant ships carrying tea would be turned away. The arrival of the *Dartmouth* in Boston Harbor with its cargo of tea on November 28th led to a stand-off between the legislature and the consignees for the tea, employees of the East India Company. Neither side was willing to back down, and the ship remained moored while the interested parties attempted to find a solution. On December 16th, Adams sensed that an attempt would be made to unload the tea. In response, a group of fifty men climbed aboard the *Dartmouth* and two other ships moored in Boston Harbor and dumped 90,000 pounds of tea into the harbor. The demonstration was soon celebrated in the press as the Boston Tea Party.

Chapter 4 – The Road to War

The Boston Tea Party shocked observers in Britain. Even parliamentarians sympathetic to the colonies, including Rockingham and Chatham, regarded it as a disgraceful criminal act. Lord North spoke for his parliamentary colleagues when he declared that the events in North America changed the nature of the debate in such a way that it was no longer a dispute about taxation, but about whether the British Crown could command any authority in the Thirteen Colonies. In the spring of 1774, Parliament passed a series of measures designed to punish Boston in order to prevent further demonstrations against British authority. The legislation limited the powers of the Massachusetts legislature, but the greatest restriction came with the Boston Port Act, which stipulated the closure of the port of Boston to commercial trade until the East India Company was compensated by the Bostonians for the destruction of the tea. News of these measures arrived in the colonies in May, and they were soon referred to as the Intolerable Acts. Samuel Adams proposed that Boston suspend trade with Britain and the British West Indies, and encouraged the rest of the colonies to follow suit. While many colonials were sympathetic to Boston's plight and recognized that they might eventually suffer the same treatment, most colonial merchants remained in favor of maintaining a trading relationship with the British.

In September and October 1774, representatives of twelve colonies met in Philadelphia at the first Continental Congress in an effort to determine a united response to the Intolerable Acts. The key grievances remained the same from ten years ago, though the mantra of no taxation without representation had been repeated so often over the previous decade that even though it was heavily contested during the Stamp Act crisis, it was taken for granted in the mid-1770s. Furthermore, by this point colonial opinion was virtually united in denying Parliament's right to make any form of legislation in the colonies. Nevertheless, the delegates found it difficult to agree on the nature of the joint colonial response to the Intolerable Acts. The delegation from Massachusetts took the most radical position, calling for an end to all trade with Britain. The Middle and Southern Colonies were less enthusiastic, being keenly aware of the damage it would do to their agricultural economies. After much negotiation, the delegates consented to an agreement on trade restrictions called the Association, which was signed on October 20th. The final days of the Congress were dedicated to drafting petitions to the king and addresses to the people of Great Britain. The delegates decided not to send a petition to Parliament, believing that it would amount to an admission of parliamentary authority over the colonies. When the delegates closed the Congress on October 26th, they agreed to meet again the following spring.

In Boston, British Governor General Thomas Gage attempted to enforce the Intolerable Acts to the best of his abilities. In October, he dissolved Massachusetts's provincial assembly in order to impose direct rule in the colony. The assembly refused to disband and relocated to Concord, some twenty miles to the west of Boston, calling itself the Provisional Congress. Under the leadership of the wealthy merchant John Hancock, the Provisional Congress assumed the duties of government and took steps to raise a militia. Confined to Boston, Gage found himself facing open rebellion. With only two regiments at his disposal, he did not feel secure in his position and requested reinforcements from London. At the same time, he advised Parliament to repeal the Intolerable Acts to diffuse the rebellion. In order to consolidate his position, Gage gave orders to seize armaments from neighboring towns in Massachusetts. Gage underestimated the determination of the colonials, and in response, militiamen marched to Boston's aid, expecting Gage to initiate hostilities against the port. Over the course of spring 1775, both sides were locked in a spiral of escalation, as each defensive action came to be regarded as an offensive action by the opposing side. On April 14th, Gage received instructions from the Earl of Dartmouth, the colonial secretary in the North ministry, to arrest the members of the Provincial Congress. Both Dartmouth and Gage knew that this would lead to war, but London was of the opinion that it was better to confront the colonials sooner rather than later. Nevertheless, the reinforcements of 20,000 men that Gage requested were not granted. The British believed that victory would come easily.

After receiving authorization from London to act against the Provisional Congress, Gage moved toward Concord. He did not aim to arrest the leaders of the Provisional Congress since most of them were in hiding, but to capture armaments to add to his limited supplies. Although the British general did all he could to conceal his preparations, they were observed by informers sympathetic to the Provisional Congress. The Boston silversmith Paul Revere was engaged as an intelligence officer for the Massachusetts militia. During the night of April 18th, 1775, once the British had finished their preparations and were preparing to march to Concord, Revere rode off to warn the leaders of the Congress, Samuel Adams and John Hancock, who were hiding in the town of Lexington to the east of Concord. Revere never uttered the words "The British are coming!" which were later attributed to him, since Revere and his comrades continued to regard themselves as British citizens. Although Revere was intercepted by British regulars on his way to Concord, others made it to Concord to warn the town of the impending British approach. Militia units from both towns were alerted and awaited orders from their commanders.

The British regulars arrived in Lexington at five o'clock on the morning of April 19th. As the drum sounded, Captain John Parker called upon seventy men drawn up in two ranks on Lexington Green. A column of British light infantrymen approached the town under the command of Major John Pitcairn. Although the militiamen were heavily outnumbered, Captain Parker ordered his men to stand firm. Parker's resolution failed him once Pitcairn urged the militia to disarm and disperse. The militia commander ordered his men to fall out, holding on to their muskets. The British officers were not satisfied by the militia's failure to disarm and repeated his instructions. During this tense standoff, a shot rang out. It is impossible to be certain whether the "shot heard round the world" came from the British regulars or the American militia. Both sides later blamed the other, and it was almost certainly accidental. In response, one of Pitcairn's subordinate officers ordered the men to fire. Pitcairn tried to stop his men from firing, but his orders were lost in the chaos and confusion of the armed confrontation. The British easily overcame the enemy fire, killing eight militiamen and wounding ten in the process. Having removed the obstacle, Pitcairn ordered his men to reform into columns as they resumed their march toward Concord.

The people of Concord had already been alerted to the movements of the British soldiers and made preparations to defend the town. Militiamen from neighboring towns rushed to its defense. The companies of militia showed little resistance against the British regulars who occupied themselves by searching for munitions. Their haphazard manner managed to cause a fire in the courthouse. The militiamen observed the smoke and were under the impression that the British intended to burn down the town. They duly resolved to attack the regulars in the town, in the process inflicting the first casualties the British army would suffer during the war. Over the course of the day, fighting took place along a sixteen-mile front, as militia companies directed their fire at the British regulars on their way back to Boston. The militiamen enjoyed a numerical advantage and had knowledge of the local terrain, but were encumbered by their lack of discipline. Under constant fire, the regulars also found it difficult to maintain their cohesion. Over the course of the entire day, the British received 273 casualties to the Americans' 95. It would become the prelude to much bloodier encounters between the two sides.

News about the battles of Lexington and Concord made its way throughout the colonies over the following days, although accounts of the battle varied in their accuracy. Although the conflict was small in scale and largely triggered by accident, the importance of the day's actions was not lost among political leaders in all thirteen colonies. Men from New England flocked to Boston to reinforce the militiamen who had taken part in the actions at Concord and Lexington. On May 10th, a force of New England militiamen commanded by Benedict Arnold seized Fort Ticonderoga in New York from the British garrison. Although the fort was dilapidated and poorly garrisoned, it was of great strategic importance due to its position between the St. Lawrence and Hudson Rivers. The New Englanders feared that continued British control of the fort might result in the cutting of communications between states on either side of the Hudson River, allowing the British to defeat the Thirteen Colonies piecemeal. The fort was also home to a large quantity of cannons which were transported to Boston.

The first major battle in the war came in June at Bunker Hill. Dissatisfied by Gage's command in Boston, Dartmouth sent three prominent generals to assist him: William Howe, John Burgoyne, and Henry Clinton. Their arrival caused the British to take more active measures by occupying Dorchester Hill overlooking Boston.

In response, the Americans occupied and fortified three hills on the Charlestown Peninsula north of Boston. Howe led the main assault on Bunker Hill and neighboring Breed's Hill. Expecting an easy victory over the colonials, Howe ordered his men to advance slowly and methodically in line formation rather than in columns. This costly tactical error impeded Howe's progress, and his men were met with defiant fire from fortified positions. Although Howe eventually took the hills as the defenders ran out of ammunition, the assault cost the British 1,000 men, including Major Pitcairn who had fought at Lexington. American casualties were far fewer at 300, but the men killed included Joseph Warren, a prominent Massachusetts political leader who had been commissioned as major general in the colonial militia.

While the British and New England forces were engaged in the bloody contest at Bunker Hill, the delegates of the Second Continental Congress were meeting in Philadelphia. The body convened on May 10th, as stipulated by the First Continental Congress seven months earlier. Following the outbreak of hostilities at Concord and Lexington, the delegates agreed that more soldiers were needed to defend the colonies. George Washington, representing Virginia, wore his militia uniform each day to the Congress to remind delegates of the military imperatives. Nevertheless, there was no agreement among the delegates on whether their ultimate objective was reconciliation with the British Empire or independence. Disagreements among the colonies were exacerbated when news of the capture of Fort Ticonderoga arrived on May 17th. The fort was located in New York, but had been captured by Connecticut men under Benedict Arnold and the Green Mountain Boys of Vermont—a militia force headed by Ethan Allen, who was instrumental in establishing Vermont as a separate political entity against the claims of New Hampshire and New York. Arnold and Allen failed to inform the authorities in New York in advance of the attack. Not only did New York feel that its territorial sovereignty had been violated by New Englanders, but the colonial authorities were still reluctant to engage in military action with the British. The Congress did all it could to ignore these conflicts between colonies in order to accelerate preparations for the war. Committees were established to secure military supplies, and on June 14th, the Congress decided to establish a Continental Army and recruit men from across the colonies to support the New Englanders around Boston. The following day they appointed George Washington as commander of the Continental Army.

While the Second Continental Congress was meeting in Philadelphia, political discussions were also taking place in London. Both King George and Parliament appear to have been surprised by the tenacity and resilience of the Americans, whom the British expected to defeat easily. On July 26th, when news of the engagement at Bunker Hill filtered through to London, North's Cabinet authorized sending 2,000 men to reinforce the army in Boston and made provisions for 20,000 men by the following spring. The popular mood was firmly in favor of war, and both the king and his prime minister were at the height of their popularity. When an emissary from the Continental Congress arrived in September to present their Olive Branch Petition to the king, requesting that he mediate between Westminster and the colonies, the king rejected it without hesitation. On October 26th, as the king made his way to Westminster for the state opening of Parliament, large crowds gathered to show their support. In his speech, George declared that America was in rebellion and that his government was determined to put the rebellion down by force. In the parliamentary debates that followed the king's speech, support for North's policy was by no means unanimous. In the Commons, a number of prominent figures including John Wilkes, Edmund Burke and Charles James Fox characterized government policy as unjust and warned that British forces were destined to be defeated by the determined Americans fighting in defense of their natural rights. The debates raged throughout the night until four in the morning, but eventually the Commons voted overwhelmingly in favor of the king's policy.

Chapter 5 – David Versus Goliath

The political decisions made in Philadelphia and London over the course of 1775 transformed the disturbances in New England into a continental war. The American Revolutionary War would also spread to Europe in subsequent years. Before considering the political and military developments in North America over the course of the war, it is important to take a closer look at the opposing forces and their relative strength, not only in terms of numbers but also by considering such factors as organization, logistics, motivation, and leadership. These factors are essential in understanding the trajectory of the war and its eventual outcome. Some of these characteristics were already apparent during the early stages of the war at Lexington, Concord, and Bunker Hill. While both sides would attempt to address their deficiencies over the course of the war to varying degrees of success, most of these factors continued to apply throughout the conflict.

At the beginning of the war, the British military presence in North America numbered little more than a couple of thousand men. By

European standards, the British standing army was not a large force. In 1775, it numbered around 36,000 men worldwide. The small size of the British army was both motivated by geography and policy. Since Britain was an island nation, it was a naval power rather than a land power. In times of peace, the Royal Navy would patrol the oceans to protect British colonial interests. In times of war, the navy served as the "wooden walls" which defended Britain, while embarking on aggressive ventures to seize the colonial possessions of rival empires. During wartime, men would be recruited to join the enlarged army, but this was a secondary consideration, and most of these men would be demobilized in peacetime. Over the course of the conflict, the British presence in North America increased to around 50,000 men in total. Recruiting and supplying an army of this size was expensive, so the British also engaged 30,000 German mercenaries, mostly from the state of Hesse. The British army was also supported by locals including 25,000 Loyalists, which were Americans who supported the British cause in the war. At any point in time, the British and their allies might field 70,000 men from Canada in the north to Florida in the South.

While the British government was required to enlarge its small regular army, Washington had to build his Continental Army from scratch. At the start of the war, it amounted to a collection of militia units recruited from New England to defend Boston. British General John Burgoyne dismissed them as a "rabble in arms." When Washington took command of the New Englanders, he could count on around 15,000 men under his disposal. This would be bolstered by the addition of 10,000 men recruited from Pennsylvania, Maryland, and Virginia by the Continental Congress. When the army was established in June 1775, new recruits would serve for one year. Few men decided to stay on in the ranks. Many simply packed their bags and went home, despite their officers' pleas. The Continental Congress raised a new army in 1776, but by 1777, it was faced with the prospect of being heavily outnumbered when the British bolstered their forces in North America with the 30,000 Hessian mercenaries. In response, the Continental Congress decided to extend terms of service of new recruits to three years and to maintain an army of 120 regiments, or around 90,000 men. By the end of the war, 200,000 men saw service in the Continental Army. The army was supported by militias which remained under the control of individual colonies.

The American Revolutionary War is often described as a war between the highly disciplined British regular army and an inexperienced American militia motivated by a glorious cause under the inspired leadership of Washington. This characterization was certainly true at the beginning of the war. Although few in number, British soldiers were highly trained and disciplined. Their predecessors won great victories over King Louis XIV (1643-1715) of France's armies during the War of the Spanish Succession. The British also achieved great success against the French during the Seven Years' War, and many officers were veterans of the conflict who once again found themselves in America. In the rulebook of 18th-century warfare, training and discipline were crucial in enabling armies to execute complicated tactical and strategic maneuvers in order to win victories on the battlefield. A highly trained army could coordinate their fire to achieve maximum impact, before charging en masse with the bayonet against enemy lines with devastating effect. Washington's forces lacked the discipline of the British, and over the course of the war, the American commander labored to impose order on his men. A Virginian aristocrat, he considered the New England soldiers too egalitarian. In Massachusetts, the officers were elected by rank and file, which hindered efforts to impose order. As soon as he arrived in Boston to take up his command, Washington personally ensured that order was maintained among his regiments at camp, a task usually reserved to junior officers in European armies, but the American commander began the war with few capable officers under his command.

Both the British and American armies encountered difficulties supplying their armies. The British government may have had the financial resources to support the war effort through the issuing of government debt, but its army was fighting several thousand miles from home. In order to supply their forces in North America, the Royal Navy had to transport men and munitions over the Atlantic. Since the British enjoyed maritime superiority and the Americans did not have an established naval force, the British were able to supply their armies without much difficulty during the initial years of the war. At the same time, the British Navy could enforce a blockade on American maritime trade. Once France joined the war against Britain, however, the French Navy was in a position to protect American ports and threaten British convoys in the Atlantic, leaving the British land forces more vulnerable. The British could count on the support of Loyalists in America to maintain their armies, but they often operated on hostile territory and dependence on the Loyalists became more difficult over time as public opinion shifted in favor of the revolutionaries.

While the logistical problems facing the British army increased over time, the Continental Army's organization became more effective during the war. When Washington took command, the army lacked basic necessities including money, armaments, clothing, and medicine. The colonial economy remained largely agrarian, so most of the gunpowder had to be smuggled from Europe. Although food was plentiful, the military camps were rife with disease. The ill-discipline in the army was accompanied by poor standards of cleanliness as the soldiers failed to wash their clothes or their cooking utensils, facilitating the spread of disease. Most of the men did not have uniforms and their officers wore few distinguishing marks. The firearms employed by the Continental Army were as varied as their clothes. As the winter of 1775 approached, Washington was well aware that his men lacked the tents and blankets to remain in the field. Without a central government, the colonies lacked the logistical capabilities to supply a field army. While the delegates of the Continental Congress agreed to furnish the Continental Army with supplies, disputes between the colonies over how much each should provide hindered progress. More than anyone else, Washington knew of the difficulties in requesting supplies from the Congress. He knew it was essential for the colonies to set aside their differences to support the war effort. Over time, the colonies managed to cooperate more effectively through the Congress to maintain and support the Continental Army, but during the early stages of the war, Washington was keenly aware that his ill-equipped and undisciplined army could disintegrate at any moment.

One of the key advantages enjoyed by Washington's forces lay in motivation and commitment to a political cause. The British army was like any other European army at the time. Its objectives were not national but dynastic. The British army fought in North America in an effort to maintain King George's rule over the Thirteen Colonies. The army was commanded by an aristocratic officer class with a tradition of service to the king and seeking military glory, but the rank and file hailed from the lowest classes in society and were usually forced into military service. For these men, even if they considered themselves loyal subjects to the king, they were not fighting for their homes but for abstract political objectives. Over the course of the war, some British soldiers realized that there was no sense in fighting and would cross the front line to join the Americans, although there was some traffic in the opposite direction in the initial stages of the war when the Continental Army frequently found itself in desperate situations. In contrast to the British regulars, Washington's army had a clear sense of what it was fighting for. The men under his command were volunteers, usually farmers and tradesmen of various descriptions. They were committed to defending their homes and their ancient rights, and committed to the glorious cause which had brought all the colonies together to fight against British tyranny. Theirs was a war necessitated by self-defense rather than imperialistic ambitions.

Another crucial aspect of the war was military leadership. The British generals were experienced and enjoyed reputations as successful military leaders during the Seven Years' War. Over the course of the war, the British employed four different commanders-in-chief: Thomas Gage was replaced by William Howe in October 1775, who gave way to Sir Henry Clinton in 1778. Clinton was replaced in turn by Guy Carleton in 1782, who was given the task of evacuating men and supplies from North America. The British commanders were reliant on orders from London, which could take more than a month to arrive. All of these commanders, trained in conventional European warfare, underestimated the resolve of the Americans and failed to adapt to the irregular forms of warfare employed by Washington's men. The commanders-in-chief were further encumbered by frosty relationships with both their subordinate generals and admirals in the Royal Navy, and frequent disagreements about strategy hindered the effective prosecution of the war. The British generals tended to move cautiously in order to maintain their lines of communication and supply, even though a decisive blow in the early stages of the war could have destroyed the Continental Army. The British also faced the perennial dilemma encountered by imperial powers seeking to pacify rebellions in their empires. Since they aimed to restore British rule over the Thirteen Colonies, the British army had to ensure that they did not alienate local populations since it would be impossible to reimpose direct rule among a hostile population even if Washington was defeated.

In contrast to the prominent military figures who commanded the British army in America, the only American general of any renown was the commander-in-chief, George Washington. Washington had seen success during the Seven Years' War and proved himself a brave officer. Nevertheless, he had little experience commanding large bodies of men—the largest unit he commanded was a regiment of less than a thousand men. However, his experience commanding the Virginia militia during the war demonstrated the necessity of imposing order in the army and in ensuring that his men were well-supplied. In his fifteen-year absence from military service Washington entered the Virginia House of Burgesses and understood the political issues at stake. He knew that his men needed no encouragement to confront the enemy, and effectively employed irregular units to distract the enemy and help him achieve greater strategic objectives. He recognized that his army was in danger of disintegration at any moment and took all measures to ensure that his army could live to fight another day. He preferred to retreat instead of risking his army against the odds, pursuing a so-called Fabian strategy.

Washington was by no means the only talented general in the Continental Army. Nathanael Greene, 33 years old at the beginning of the war, had only six months' military experience when appointed to the rank of brigadier general. His strategic understanding and commitment to the American cause soon won him promotion to major general in 1776. Henry Knox, aged 25 in 1775, was a skilled artilleryman who managed to bring the guns from Ticonderoga to Boston in the winter of 1775. He would later become the artillery commander in the Continental Army and play a crucial role at the decisive Siege of Yorktown. British generals often advanced through the ranks through seniority and favors to the king. While connections also mattered in the Continental Army, talented American officers were often promoted to senior ranks for the successes they achieved on the battlefield.

Chapter 6 – Independence

When the Second Continental Congress met in the spring of 1775, most of the delegates supported reconciliation with the British. The increasing intensity of the conflict over the course of the year strengthened the desire for independence. The decisions made by Parliament and the North ministry to declare America in rebellion also led many to conclude that reconciliation was impossible. Despite their professed loyalty to the king, the delegates of the Continental Congress and the officers of the Continental Army were identified as traitors to the king, and their prospects in the event of a reconciliation with Britain would have been bleak.

Despite these developments, the Congress refrained from declaring independence at the beginning of 1776. Popular opinion in the Thirteen Colonies was split. When the war began, around a third of the American people were Patriots who supported the revolutionary cause. Another third were Loyalists who identified themselves with their British colonial masters. The remaining third were moderates who did not have strong political opinions and were primarily concerned about their personal interests. At the beginning of the war, this group favored reconciliation with the British and the preservation of the existing order, but over the course of time, they recognized the increasing brutality of British troops and understood that the British were seeking retribution on America.

The cause of independence was effectively advanced in the court of public opinion by the publication of *Common Sense* by Thomas Paine. An Englishman who had only been in America for a little more than a year, Paine was not a natural spokesman for the cause of American independence. After repeated failures in several trades in England, Paine crossed the Atlantic on the recommendation of Benjamin Franklin in late 1774, and soon found himself writing press articles in Pennsylvania newspapers. In *Common Sense*, a political pamphlet published in January 1776, Paine attacked the British constitution for being a vehicle for tyranny. He argued that the institution of monarchy contravened both natural rights and Christian teachings. In a memorable passage criticizing the principle of hereditary succession that governed most European polities of the time, Paine remarked that nature "disapproves of it, otherwise she would not so frequently turn it into ridicule by giving mankind an Ass for a Lion." Based on these precepts, the Americans should not be aiming to restore whatever ancient liberties they enjoyed under the British constitution, but they should declare independence and establish a polity based on natural rights. Some of these arguments had been expressed in earlier debates, but no one expressed it with the eloquence and wit of Thomas Paine. Within a few months, more than 100,000 copies of *Common Sense* appeared across the colonies. Through his writing, Paine promoted the question of independence to the top of the political agenda.

Common Sense emboldened the advocates for independence in the Continental Congress. Independence would not only galvanize the Continental Army behind a great cause, but would also enable Americans to enter alliances with foreign states. By April, colonial legislatures across the Thirteen Colonies authorized their delegates at

Congress to seek a confederation which would bring them together and break off relations with the British Crown. The most radical pro-independent delegates included the cousins Samuel and John Adams from Massachusetts, and the brothers Francis Lee and Richard Henry Lee of Virginia. On June 6th,1776, Richard Henry Lee presented a resolution which proposed the dissolution of relations between the united colonies and the British Crown. The resolution also proposed that Congress seek measures to secure foreign assistance and to form a confederation between the colonies. When the proposal was debated by Congress, New England and Virginia were in favor of independence, while the Middle Colonies indicated that the time was not ripe, although they would support independence once the people demanded it. Congress opted to postpone discussions to July 1st and appointed committees to consider the proposals for independence, foreign alliances, and a confederation.

The five-man committee tasked with preparing a declaration of independence included Benjamin Franklin and John Adams, but the document was mainly drafted by the 33-year-old Thomas Jefferson. A Virginia gentleman, Jefferson was related through his mother's side to the Randolph family, one of the most prominent families in Virginia. His mother's cousin Peyton Randolph served as the first president of the Continental Congress before his death in October 1775. As a young man, Jefferson proved to be an excellent student with a particular affinity for Greek and Latin. He graduated from William and Mary College in 1762 before embarking on a career as a lawyer. In 1769, he was elected to the House of Burgesses. In 1774, Jefferson authored *A Summary View of the Rights of British America* in response to the Intolerable Acts. He argued that the people of America had the right to govern themselves and that the Thirteen Colonies were independent from British rule since the foundation of the individual colonies. Jefferson's tract was debated at the First Continental Congress, and he himself was elected to the Second Continental Congress in May 1775.

Jefferson completed his draft of the Declaration of Independence on June 28th, and the document was slightly amended by Adams and Franklin. On July 1st, the Congress voted on the issue of independence. Nine colonies voted in favor, Pennsylvania and South Carolina voted against, Delaware's delegation was split, and New York was not yet authorized by its colonial legislature to vote on the question. The following day, the Congress held another vote in which Pennsylvania, South Carolina, and Delaware voted in favor of independence with only New York remaining uncommitted. Following the landmark vote, John Adams wrote that July 2nd would be recognized by future generations as the day that America broke free from the British Empire. In fact, the Declaration of Independence would not be passed until July 4th, after it was analyzed line by line and approved after many amendments which toned down some of Jefferson's more radical denunciations. It was this day, the Fourth of July, which would be celebrated as Independence Day in the United States of America.

In its introduction, the Declaration of Independence established the Thirteen Colonies as the United States of America. In his famous preamble, Jefferson stated the creed of this new nation: "We hold these truths to be self-evident, that all men are created equal, that they are endowed by their Creator with certain unalienable Rights, that among these are Life, Liberty and the pursuit of Happiness." Although the equality of men was certainly a revolutionary doctrine for the time, both women and slaves were not included in Jefferson's phrasing. The preamble continues to demonstrate that revolution is permissible when a tyrannical government harms the people's natural and God-given rights. Much of the document is dedicated to outlining a list of King George's tyrannical injustices including the suppression of colonial legislative bodies, imposing taxation without consent, and the use of armed force in America. Such injustices made the king "unfit to be the ruler of a free people." This argument was inspired by the liberal philosopher John Locke's concept of a social contract between a monarch and his subjects. A tyrannical monarch was said to have broken the social contract and thus been deprived of political legitimacy. The Declaration continues with a denunciation of the British government in its insistence to impose parliamentary authority in the Thirteen Colonies, before concluding with a statement declaring that the Thirteen Colonies were free and independent states "absolved from all allegiance to the British Crown" and therefore had the authority to make war and peace, and regulate commerce in the fashion of other independent states. The Declaration was signed by 56 men, although some of them were not present on July 4th and added their signatures on later dates, when New York's delegates were finally authorized to vote in favor of independence.

The publication of the Declaration of Independence on July 7th had a galvanizing effect on both the people and the army of the newly-established United States of America. Printing presses worked unceasingly to distribute copies of the document across the country. Spontaneous celebrations broke out on July 6th, when the Continental Army first learned of the decisive vote in favor of independence four days earlier. On July 9th, Washington gave orders for the Declaration to be read aloud to ranks of soldiers gathered on parade grounds. Not only did Jefferson's words stir the hearts of the rank and file who were convinced of the righteousness of their cause, but in declaring independence, the Continental Congress had committed treason against their king. The price of defeat and surrender would be so great that there could be no turning back in their dedication to their cause. Washington's army was no longer fighting for their rights as Englishmen but for a new nation founded on the principles of liberty and equality. After the formal readings on July 9th, soldiers and townspeople expressed their enthusiasm by pulling down an equestrian statue of George III. They then hacked off the head and placed it on a spike. Not all people supported independence, but those who rejected it found themselves in a diminishing minority.

Once the Americans had declared independence from Britain, they had to prove that they could function effectively as an independent entity. The United States of America was a political experiment, and it was by no means certain that the experiment would succeed. The United States was a union of thirteen states, each of which had new governments and political institutions of their own. In order to support the Continental Army and make treaties of alliance against the British Empire, the United States needed a central political authority. As British colonies, relationships between states were defined by a sense of mutual mistrust, especially when territorial claims overlapped. The struggle with Britain enabled the Americans to discover that they had more in common than they initially thought, but differences in the socio-economic character of the states contributed to political differences. Even when delegates in Congress came to agreement on measures such as the boycott of British trade in 1774, these measures would have to be implemented by local and colonial authorities.

The task of drafting a plan of union was entrusted to John Dickinson, who chaired the congressional committee looking into the question. A delegate from Pennsylvania, Dickinson had opposed declaring independence before such a union could be established, believing it would risk conflict between the colonies. The Articles of Confederation and Perpetual Union drafted by Dickinson aimed to balance the interests of individual states with the need for high-level cooperation to support the war against the British. The main part of the document consisted of thirteen articles asserting the sovereignty of the states and detailing their obligations to the union. Each state, depending on population, would choose two to seven delegates for the Congress of the Confederation, but each state would have one vote and therefore each state, big or small, would be given an equal voice. Any decision needed nine votes to agree, and any change in the Articles needed all states to agree. The head of state would be a president, who was limited to serving one year in each three-year congressional term. Most of the powers of Congress were laid out in

Article IX of the document. Among the powers accorded to Congress was the right to make war and peace and enter diplomatic agreements, to set weights and measures, and to regulate post and the armed forces. The Congress could not tax or draft people into the military, but would determine how much each state had to send to the common treasury and how many men each state was obliged to send to the Continental Army.

Dickinson's plan was presented to the Continental Congress on July 12th, but the subject of a union between the states was so contentious that Congress would continue to debate the issue for more than a year. These debates revolved around three key issues: division of powers between states and the confederation, representation of states in Congress, and contributions of the states to the union. Moreover, claims of the western lands were made by several states who hoped to expand their own territories and further their economic interests. Maryland was keen to ensure that all states would cede their claims to the western territories to the Union, and resisted ratification even though the twelve other states had done so by February 1779. Maryland eventually ratified the Articles in February 1781, and in March, they were proclaimed as the law of the United States. Even before the ratification of the document by all the states, the Articles of Confederation served as the framework for cooperation between the individual states. The Second Continental Congress continued to meet in order to coordinate the war effort, despite political differences between the states. The support of Congress was necessary for Washington to continue fighting the war since the Continental Army was fighting for its survival.

Chapter 7 – Washington on the Ropes

The military developments during the first half of 1776 were positive for the Continental Army. After an ill-fated attempt to invade Canada at the end of 1775, Washington decided to turn his attention toward the siege of Boston. Although the Americans outnumbered the British, the defenders were behind well-fortified lines and easily supplied by the navy through Boston Harbor. During the winter of 1775, Colonel Henry Knox successfully hauled fifty-six cannons from Fort Ticonderoga to the outskirts of Boston, a journey of almost 300 miles across frozen rivers. Knox personally supervised the mission and did not lose a single gun in transit, bringing the guns to the siege camp outside Boston in late January 1776. For this miraculous operation, Washington immediately appointed Knox to command the artillery in the Continental Army. Strengthened with these extra guns, Washington hoped to immediately launch an assault on British lines but was overruled by his subordinates.

Instead, Washington's war council adopted a plan to occupy the Dorchester Heights and entice General Howe's army out of their fortifications. Washington's men successfully occupied the Heights during the night of March 4th-5th. The guns from Ticonderoga could now be trained on the British fleet in Boston Harbor, which provided for Howe's only line of retreat. The heavy bombardment forced Howe to withdraw from Boston and sail to Halifax, Nova Scotia on March 17th.

Although the British had retreated to Canada to reorganize their forces, Washington knew that Howe would eventually move on New York, a city of vital strategic importance. If the British were to occupy New York and control the Hudson River, the United States would be divided into two, and Howe could concentrate his forces to conquer and subdue each portion in turn. With these considerations in mind, after Boston was firmly in American hands, Washington led an army of 18,000 men to New York and arrived at the beginning of April, setting up headquarters at the end of Broadway. He could see that unlike Boston, the Patriots were at a political and strategic disadvantage in New York. While most Bostonians eagerly supported the revolution, not least because their city was specifically targeted by Parliament, New Yorkers were more inclined to remain loyal to the British Crown. Furthermore, with British control of the seas, the Americans would not be able to hold onto the city for long. Nevertheless, there was a political imperative for the Continental Army to make a stand in New York, demonstrating to the Patriots in New York that their city would not be abandoned without a fight. Washington ordered fortifications to be built on Brooklyn Heights overlooking Long Island to the south of the city.

By the end of June, British ships began arriving at Staten Island commanded by Admiral Lord Richard Howe, General Howe's brother. General Howe himself landed on July 2nd, 1776, the same day the Continental Congress voted to declare independence. Although news of the decision invigorated Washington's army, the Americans remained on the back foot. The 120 cannons which Knox had installed on the banks of the Hudson did nothing to prevent Admiral Howe's flagship, the HMS *Eagle*, from entering New York in all its majesty. The Howes had been appointed peace commissioners by Parliament and offered talks with Washington. Their reluctance to address Washington by his title of general led to two refusals, until finally on July 20th, General Washington met with the British. Both sides knew it was unrealistic to expect a peaceful outcome, but both sides believed it was worth trying for political reasons. Washington refused to consider any pardon from the king by insisting that the Americans had done no wrong in defending their liberties. Formalities over, both sides prepared for war. Howe had 32,000 men under his command, including a large contingent of Hessian mercenaries. Washington had no indication of the direction of attack, and despite being outnumbered, decided to divide his forces between Brooklyn and Manhattan, which proved to be a grave tactical error. The assault began on August 23rd and reached its climax on August 27th. The British launched an attack on the Brooklyn Heights while a Hessian force outflanked the American lines and attacked from the rear. In the confusion, some of Washington's men retreated in disorder, while the remaining men valiantly fought on. Washington's attempts to restore order were in vain. The Battle of Brooklyn had been a disastrous defeat for the Continental Army, which sustained casualties of 1,500 men.

Washington knew he had to abandon the Heights, but any attempt to withdraw his men to Manhattan in broad daylight would amount to a suicide mission. Instead, he ordered his men to requisition any boats they could get their hands on to prepare for an evacuation at night. On the night of August 29th, the evacuation began. Although by daybreak not all the Americans had evacuated from Brooklyn, a dense fog continued to shield their retreat. The British camp was filled with a sense of relief that the Americans had evacuated their positions voluntarily, and Howe decided to consolidate his position. Had he carried on the pursuit, he could have brought ruin to Washington's army and the entire American cause. Despite losing many men from desertion in the aftermath of the defeat at Brooklyn, Washington lived to fight another day. The Continentals fought a series of rearguard actions along the Hudson River, retreating at every step while sustaining and inflicting casualties along the way.

The New York campaign had been a disaster, which persuaded Congress to raise 80,000 more men for the Continental Army. The recruiting of men needed time which Washington lacked. His army of 3,500 men retreated to New Jersey in anticipation of an attack on Philadelphia. Thomas Paine, in a series of pamphlets titled *The American Crisis*, described the mood of the Patriots with the famous opening line, "These are the times that try men's souls." By the end of November, Washington crossed the Delaware River to the relative security of Pennsylvania. At this point, Howe decided to halt his pursuit, retaining a 1,500-man garrison of Hessians at Trenton across the Delaware. After receiving reinforcements, Washington could only count on 6,000 men fit for duty. Nevertheless, Washington resolved to counterattack. Early on the morning of December 26th, just after Christmas, Washington crossed the Delaware and surprised the Hessian garrison, winning an important victory and capturing 1,000 prisoners. The Americans followed up this victory by defeating the British garrison at Princeton before taking up winter quarters at the beginning of 1777. In six months, Washington had relinquished New York, which remained in British hands until the end of the war, but he successfully held onto New Jersey, preserved his army, and could afford to celebrate some successes at the end of the year which restored hope among Patriots that the war could be won.

Despite the successes in late 1776, the Continental Army remained on the defensive. The key objective was the defense of Pennsylvania and Philadelphia, the de facto capital of the United States. In fact, in December 1776, the Continental Congress had already evacuated to Baltimore, Maryland to seek greater security. Once Washington successfully prevented Howe from entering Pennsylvania, the Congress returned to Philadelphia in March 1777. Howe believed the key strategic objective was to destroy Washington's army, and in the spring, he attempted in vain to entice Washington to an open battle in New Jersey. With Washington unwilling to fall into his trap, Howe returned to New York before setting sail in mid-August. Washington guessed that Howe would attempt to land a force on the Delaware River and attack Philadelphia. While Howe was indeed targeting Philadelphia, he landed instead on the Chesapeake in Maryland before marching north. The Continental Army moved to intercept the British march to Philadelphia by establishing headquarters at Wilmington, Delaware. The two armies clashed at Brandywine Creek on September 11th, where Washington's army was once again outflanked by Howe. Although the Continentals fought with greater tenacity than at Brooklyn a year earlier, by the end of the bloody melee, they retreated in disorder.

Once again, the British had won a significant victory over the Americans, but once again Washington managed to prevent his army from disintegrating. There followed weeks of maneuvering during which the Continental Army sought to keep itself between Howe and Philadelphia. As Washington was shifting his army left and right to cover Howe's movements, part of his army stationed in Paoli, some twenty miles to the northwest of Philadelphia, was surprised by the British during the night and 300 Continentals were killed by British bayonets. The Paoli Massacre prompted Washington to be more careful in his maneuvers, but this allowed Howe to enter Philadelphia on September 26th, forcing the Continental Congress to flee once again, eventually establishing temporary premises at York, a hundred miles to the west of Philadelphia. While this was a significant setback, Washington's army remained intact, and the American commander intended on retaking the city as soon as possible. On October 4th, he attacked Howe's army at Germantown, some five miles to the northwest of Philadelphia. Washington sent four forces along four separate roads which converged on Germantown and an unsuspecting Howe. Although the American plan looked impressive on paper, the separate forces failed to coordinate their attacks effectively. The fact that the battlefield was covered in fog resulted in two of the American columns firing at each other before they discovered their mistake. The British took advantage of the confusion in American ranks and launched a successful counterattack. The Continental Army's defeat at Germantown would prevent the Americans from recapturing Philadelphia until the following year. Washington led his army of 12,000 men to winter quarters at Valley Forge, 20 miles northwest of Philadelphia to reorganize his army.

While Washington's main army suffered defeat in Pennsylvania, American forces in upstate New York enjoyed greater success. With New York City in British hands, the British could seize control of the Hudson River Valley and separate New England from the rest of the United States. This was the plan formulated by General John Burgoyne and adopted by the British government in the spring of 1777. Burgoyne would move south from Canada into upstate New York, while a second force under the command of General Barry St. Leger, would move east from Ontario. Burgoyne also counted on Howe to distract the Continentals in New England. The three forces would meet in Albany—either to destroy Washington's army in tandem or to cut the United States in two. On July 1st, Burgoyne successfully recaptured Fort Ticonderoga with 8,000 men, and continued toward Albany, confronted with increasing numbers of American troops on the way, some of them sent as reinforcements from Washington's army. Burgoyne had expected assistance from Howe, but the senior general turned his attention to Philadelphia, leaving Burgoyne reliant on St. Leger for support. By the beginning of August, St. Leger was besieging Fort Stanwix on the Mohawk River, a hundred miles west of Albany in upstate New York. Two American relief columns hurried to lift the siege, and the arrival of the second under Benedict Arnold resulted in British withdrawal. St. Leger hoped to rejoin with Burgoyne's army via Canada, but Burgoyne was forced to carry on to Albany on his own.

Strategically isolated, Burgoyne staked his army in battle against a force of 9,000 Americans under the command of General Horatio Gates, who served as commander of the Continental Army in the northern sector. Gates' army took up a position on Bemis Heights, some ten miles south of Saratoga. The position was fortified by Tadeusz Kosciuszko, a skilled Polish military engineer. On September 19th, Burgoyne's army attacked Gates' left flank at Freeman's Farm, forcing the enemy to fall back at great cost. . A unit of 500 riflemen under the command of Colonel Daniel Morgan targeted the officers in the British army and inflicted important casualties. Burgoyne would continue his attack on the Heights on October 7th, but by this point the Continental Army was more than twice the size of the British contingent. Once again, Morgan's riflemen inflicted great damage on the British, and Burgoyne himself was almost killed by the sharpshooters. The accurate fire from the Continentals broke the spirit of the British attackers, who retreated back to their lines. Seizing the opportunity, Benedict Arnold led his New England men in an unauthorized attack on the retreating British and secured a famous victory. Burgoyne and his army would surrender on October 17th, leaving the British general to return home disgraced and his army to remain in captivity until the end of the war. Meanwhile, Gates was celebrated as the victor of Saratoga, and some sections of the Continental Army believed he should replace Washington as commander-in-chief.

Chapter 8 – The International Dimension

By late 1777, the American Revolutionary War assumed an international dimension. Britain and France continued to be engaged in their struggle for global hegemony which spanned the 18th century. As hostilities broke out between the British and Americans, France looked to exploit Britain's vulnerability and exact revenge for their defeat during the Seven Years' War. The American revolutionaries were keen to establish an alliance with France following the outbreak of war at Lexington and Concord, and sent several agents to Paris to negotiate a treaty of alliance with France. In March 1776, Silas Deane of Connecticut had been sent by Congress to Paris on a secret mission to negotiate with the French foreign minister, the Comte de Vergennes. In December, he was joined by Benjamin Franklin and Arthur Lee, now in an official capacity as the American diplomatic delegation in France. John Adams would join the trio in the following March. Despite such illustrious personalities representing the American cause, the French were reluctant to formally enter the war. After all, King Louis XVI (1774-91) of France was a crowned monarch who was hesitant to sanction a republican revolution. The French were also concerned about whether the Continental Army could sustain the war. Were Washington to be defeated decisively, France would find itself alone against Britain, allowing the British to concentrate their armed forces against French possessions around the world. News of the American victory in the Saratoga campaign reached Europe in December 1777. Vergennes was sufficiently confident that the Americans were not about to collapse and stood a real chance of winning the war, so he acquiesced to the offer of alliance.

Even before the alliance was formally brokered between France and the nascent United States, army officers from continental Europe were already making their way to North America to enlist in the Continental Army. The Polish military engineer Tadeusz Kosciuszko enlisted in August 1776, and the fortifications he designed enabled the victories at Saratoga against Burgoyne. His compatriot Kazimierz Pulaski, together with the Hungarian hussar (Central European light cavalry) Mihaly Kovats, were instrumental in the creation of cavalry units in the Continental Army. The Prussian General Baron Friedrich Wilhelm von Steuben would arrive in North America at the end of 1777 and was responsible for drilling and training Washington's army in European methods of warfare. By far the most influential foreign officer serving in the Continental Army over the course of the war was Gilbert du Motier, Marquis de Lafayette. Seeking military glory and motivated by the hostility toward Britain, Lafayette traveled to North America at his own expense against the wishes of his family and the French king. After his arrival in July 1777, he was commissioned as a major general in the Continental Army and soon established a close friendship with Washington. He first saw battle at Brandywine, where he received a wound in the leg but continued to issue orders and organize the orderly retreat of the Continental Army. Lafayette served on

Washington's staff and shared his privations in the winter of 1777 as the army was encamped in Valley Forge. Once the French formally joined the war in February 1778, Lafayette would prove invaluable as a liaison officer between the Continental Army and the French Navy.

The Treaties of Amity and Commerce and of Alliance between France and the United States were signed in February 1778. The two parties agreed that territorial conquests in North America would be transferred to the United States, while any gains in the Caribbean would pass to France. Most importantly, the two parties agreed not to make a separate peace with Britain. The Franco-American alliance transformed the strategic considerations of the war. The British had previously been able to supply a large army in North America without much difficulty due to its control of the seas. In comparison to the formidable Royal Navy, the naval forces of the American revolutionaries were practically nonexistent. In 1776, the Continental Navy had 27 ships in contrast to the British Navy's 270, and the gap would increase over the course of the war. Nevertheless, British commerce was constantly targeted by American merchant ships, which turned to privateering during the war. Privateering was sanctioned by both the Continental Congress and the individual states, and as many as 70,000 men may have been involved in privateering efforts against British shipping. By the end of 1777, American privateers had taken 560 British merchant vessels conducting trade across the Atlantic. The exploits of John Paul Jones, a naval captain in the Continental Navy, were particularly celebrated. His most famous action came in 1779 at the Battle of Flamborough Head, off the English coast, when he forced the surrender of the British frigate HMS *Serapis* while his own ship, the *Bonhomme Richard*, was already sinking.

While American privateers proved a nuisance for British authorities, French entry in the war brought with it the prospect of the French Navy threatening British supremacy in the American seaboard. The authorities in London therefore switched their attention to the French and proposed to seize the French island of St. Lucia in the West Indies. Not only could the British take control of the lucrative commerce in the Caribbean, but the French Navy would be distracted from their objective of supporting the American forces. Before launching any offensive operations, the British had to decide what to do with the French fleet. The main French fleet was based at Brest on the west coast of France, while a second force under the Comte d'Estaing was being furnished in Toulon on the Mediterranean. The British government and naval command were divided about the best course of action since the navy, poorly maintained since the end of the Seven Years' War, could not maintain an effective blockade of the French ports. Admiral Augustus Keppel, commander of the home fleet, preferred to protect against the prospect of an invasion of the British Isles. This allowed d'Estaing's fleet to sail unopposed to North America, arriving in New York by July 1778 to blockade Admiral Howe's fleet.

D'Estaing's arrival in the North American seaboard was a major setback for the British, although the combined operations between the French Navy and the Continental Army in the second half of 1778 did not achieve much success. Nevertheless, as long as France continued to be part of the war, London would have to protect against invasion of British shores. Although an inconclusive engagement between Admiral Keppel and the Brest fleet under the Comte d'Orvilliers near Ushant in July 1778 ensured that Britain would be safe from invasion for the remainder of the year, the threat of invasion loomed even larger the following year. Spain entered the war in April 1779, not so much as to assist the American revolutionaries, but to recapture Gibraltar from the British. In June, Spanish forces began to lay siege to Gibraltar. Although the British managed to keep Gibraltar well-supplied, an allied Franco-Spanish fleet was threatening to mount an invasion of England. A fleet of 66 ships of the line sailed up the English Channel seeking to distract the Royal Navy, while an army of 40,000 men would be ferried across the channel by 400 transport ships. The appearance of this armada on

August 14th alarmed the British, though a fleet of more than thirty ships under the command of Admiral Sir Charles Hardy managed to shadow the enemy fleet. A combination of poor coordination, poor weather, and sickness among the allied crew forced the allied fleet to abandon its venture. Once again, the British shores were secure from invasion, and the French and Spanish did not plan an invasion during the remainder of the war.

Although the British were undoubtedly concerned about French efforts to launch an invasion of Britain, the Royal Navy continued to take part in offensive operations. In accordance with the new strategy adopted in the summer of 1778, a British convoy sailed from New Jersey toward the West Indies with 5,000 men under the command of General James Grant with the task of capturing St. Lucia from the French. On December 14th, the British fleet stationed in the West Indies under the command of Admiral Samuel Barrington defeated d'Estaing's larger fleet, and by December 29th the French surrendered possession of the island to the British. Despite this British success, d'Estaing's fleet continued to enjoy numerical superiority in 1779, and the French successfully seized St. Vincent and Grenada from the British in the summer. A British fleet under Admiral John Byron attacked d'Estaing as the French admiral was sailing away from Grenada, but suffered a heavy defeat in the process. The Battle of Grenada on July 6th was the Royal Navy's worst defeat in almost a century, with Byron losing a thousand men in the engagement. The war in the West Indies would eventually also bring in the Spanish and the Dutch, and the fighting would continue until 1783, after military operations in North America were already concluded.

The distractions caused by the French and Spanish fleets increased the vulnerability of British commerce to American privateers. Between 1777 and 1780, American privateers managed to capture another 1,000 British merchant vessels. Although the Royal Navy managed to maintain control of the American seaboard for much of 1778-80, they continued to experience difficulties supplying their armies. On July 27th, 1780, a large British convoy set sail from Portsmouth destined for North America, escorted by Captain Sir John Moutray's HMS *Ramillies* and two frigates. The convoy of 63 merchant ships carried £1,000,000 of gold, together with 80,000 muskets, 294 artillery pieces, and other equipment intended for the army of 40,000 men in North America. On August 9th, 1780, while the convoy was sailing past the Azores, it was intercepted by a Franco-Spanish fleet commanded by Luis de Cordova. 55 of the British merchant ships mistook the Spanish flagship for the HMS *Ramillies* and were captured by Cordova. The Spanish took more than three thousand British prisoners, and the disaster bankrupted marine insurance underwriters throughout Europe.

Although the British fleet remained the largest in the world, it was unable to patrol the seas effectively against French, Spanish, Dutch, and American hostility. The British authorities had to decide which sectors to prioritize. Unlike in the Seven Years' War, the British could no longer rely on a continental ally to distract its European enemies. Prussia remained neutral as Frederick the Great approached his twilight years. The aging Frederick was well aware that his kingdom had almost been destroyed during the Seven Years' War and did not wish to risk his earlier territorial gains. The British requested an alliance and 20,000 troops from Russia, but Empress Catherine the Great (1762-96) disliked George III and believed the British only had themselves to blame for the revolution in their American colonies. Any hope of winning Catherine's goodwill was lost when the British adopted controversial countermeasures to confiscate neutral shipping which they suspected of carrying contraband to support the American revolutionaries. These measures infuriated Catherine the Great as Russian ships were routinely searched by British naval officers. In March 1780, she issued a Declaration of Armed Neutrality to protect the interests of neutral shipping. The declaration established the rights of neutral vessels in war and provided for their armed protection in case such rights were infringed. Catherine invited other European nations to join a League of Armed Neutrality. By 1781, Denmark, Sweden, Austria, and Prussia joined the League. Although it did not discriminate between American and British interference in neutral shipping, armed neutrality favored the American cause. Faced with armed neutrality, the Royal Navy could do nothing to prevent French and Dutch ships from flying the Russian flag and entering American ports, bringing supplies to the states. By establishing the League, Catherine had effectively recognized the United States as its own independent state on an equal basis with the British, rather than as rebellious provinces of the British Empire.

Chapter 9 – War in the South

The failure of Burgoyne's strategy in Canada, coupled with the French alliance with the American revolutionaries, forced the British to adopt a new plan. In May 1778, Howe relinquished his command to Sir Henry Clinton. Lord George Germain, who had succeeded the Earl of Dartmouth as colonial secretary in 1775, ordered Clinton to evacuate Philadelphia and return to New York. Clinton and his army would then move by sea to attack the Southern states. This new strategy seemed sensible and to play to British advantages. There was no longer any sense in conducting a land campaign in the hostile territory of the Northern states, especially as it became increasingly difficult to supply the army across the Atlantic. Instead, the army would conduct joint operations with the Royal Navy, which continued local superiority in the American seaboard, allowing the army to operate more effectively in the friendlier South. The Southern Colonies of Georgia and South Carolina were dominated by landowners whose commercial interests were limited. They were also younger colonies and had less time to develop a separate identity from their British imperial masters. The British expected to link up with Loyalists in the South and conduct joint operations against the Patriots. This force would gather strength as it moved northward to North Carolina and Virginia. The British expected that American revolutionary sentiment would be dampened by British reconquest of the South, and the war could still be won.

Clinton's army duly evacuated Philadelphia in June 1778, allowing the Continental Congress to return to its former seat by the beginning of July. 3,000 Loyalists were evacuated to New York by Admiral Howe's fleet, but Clinton's army of 10,000 men would march to the city by land. As the British withdrew, Washington and his generals debated what to do next. General Charles Lee, Washington's deputy, argued that the Continentals should allow the British to withdraw and not risk their army in field engagements, while foreign officers, including Steuben and Lafayette, encouraged Washington to assume the offensive and attack Clinton's exposed supply train. Washington eventually decided to seek battle, handing the command of the vanguard to General Lee at the latter's request. Washington's men caught up with the British at Monmouth Court House in New Jersey. Reluctant to go on the offensive, Lee introduced units at a steady pace and allowed the British rearguard under General Charles Cornwallis to seize the initiative and beat back Lee's vanguard. Only the arrival of Washington and Lafayette restored order and discipline, allowing the Continentals to regroup and push Cornwallis backward. The battle ended Lee's military career, but enhanced the reputations of Washington and Lafayette. The British continued to New York without further harassment, arriving in mid-July. Clinton's arrival in New York in mid-July coincided with the appearance of d'Estaing's fleet outside the harbor. The inability of the French ships to pass through the shallow bar of New York Harbor prevented operations against Lord Howe's fleet. A combined amphibious operation against Newport, Rhode Island also came to nothing. The Franco-American alliance at sea had yet to bear fruit.

Unlike in previous years, hostilities continued throughout the winter. Clinton initiated operations against the South at the end of 1778. In November, in addition to the 5,000 men he sent to seize St. Lucia, Clinton dispatched 3,500 men under the command of Lieutenant Colonel Archibald Campbell on an invasion of Georgia, the southernmost state. Campbell landed in Georgia on December 23rd and captured the town of Savannah on the 29th. Over the course of the following month, Campbell joined forces with General Augustine Prevost to take control of Georgia. The success of the British armies mobilized the Loyalist militia who joined the British regulars as they moved north to South Carolina. Although the British expeditionary force had seen success, Clinton stayed in New York for much of 1779. London was far more concerned about the prospect of Franco-Spanish invasion. Moreover, debates about the conduct of the war dominated political activity in Parliament. The recalled William Howe defended himself and his brother against accusations that he had been lacking in aggression as commander-in-chief of British forces in America. The British military establishment was split between whether the logistical challenges in America were insurmountable, or whether the majority of Americans remained loyal subjects to King George who would provide material support to the British military presence. The debates continued in the public press and demonstrated that support for the war was ebbing away.

Military operations in the American South resumed near the end of the year, when the Continental Army attempted to retake Savannah, assisted by Patriot militia and d'Estaing's fleet, in September. The failure of this operation prompted Clinton to bring his army south. On December 26th, 1779, Clinton left New York with 8,000 men destined for South Carolina. The target was the port of Charleston, the largest city in the southern states with a population of 12,000 citizens. The British began to lay siege on the city in late March. Clinton intended to lay siege to the city with the assistance of the Royal Navy, but disagreements with Admiral Mariot Arbuthnot obligated Clinton to cut off the city without the navy's aid. On April

21st, 1780, the American garrison, under the command of General Benjamin Lincoln, offered to surrender if the Continentals could be allowed to leave the city on their own terms, but this was refused by the British commander. Effective artillery bombardment from the British forced Lincoln to surrender—this time with his men taken into captivity and their arms confiscated. After overseeing the capture of Charleston, Clinton returned to New York and left Cornwallis in command. The latter was given orders to capture the Carolinas before invading Virginia, coordinating an attack with a British force driving south from New York.

The British regulars under Cornwallis, supported by Loyalist militia, successfully overran South Carolina within three months. During this period, a guerrilla war was conducted by militias from both sides, which would characterize the war in the South throughout 1780 and into the following year. Meanwhile, the Continental Army appointed General Horatio Gates, the victor of Saratoga, to command the army in the South. The army Gates was to command consisted of 1,400 Continentals from Delaware and Maryland headed by Johann de Kalb, a Bavarian general who had been in the service of the king of France. This force was reinforced by 2,500 militiamen from North Carolina and Virginia. In August, Gates led this army to Camden, where Cornwallis had established his supply depot in South Carolina. Gates believed that the British force was much smaller than his own, but after receiving reinforcements, Cornwallis could count on 2,000 men. Despite the faulty intelligence, Gates felt compelled to attack and opened battle on August 16th. The encounter was a disaster for the American force. The Virginian and North Carolinian militiamen had been deployed opposite Cornwallis' best troops. The well-disciplined British infantry fired on the advancing Virginia militiamen, who soon panicked and fled the field of battle along with the North Carolinian units, leaving de Kalb's men dangerously exposed. De Kalb himself valiantly fought on until he collapsed from his wounds, dying three days later in British captivity.

The guerilla war between British and American militia continued in the aftermath of Camden. Lieutenant Colonel Banastre Tarleton gained special notoriety for his conduct of this irregular warfare in the South. Tarleton was the commander of the British Legion, a Loyalist force of cavalry and light infantry, and who had played a crucial role in the siege of Charleston. The most notorious act involving Tarleton's men came in the aftermath of the Battle of Waxhaws at the end of May. The Legion defeated a contingent of 400 Continentals under Abraham Buford, whose inexperienced troops fled in the wake of the fearsome Loyalist cavalry. When Buford brought out a white flag with the intention to surrender, Tarleton's men continued their attack and slaughtered over 100 Continentals. Although most contemporary accounts suggest that Tarleton did not give such orders since he had been trapped under his dead horse during the initial stages of the battle, Tarleton and the British Legion gained a reputation for being merciless. The incident at Waxhaws inflamed passions on both sides and contributed to a bloody guerrilla war in which no quarter was given on either side. Cornwallis had handed the task of pacifying South Carolina to Major Patrick Ferguson and a militia force of 1,000 men. Although Ferguson had been largely successful in clearing the area of enemy militia, the Patriots received word of his intention of laying waste to the country and recruited some 1,000 men themselves to confront Ferguson. They surprised and defeated Ferguson at King's Mountain on October 7th. The victorious Patriots refused to accept the surrender of the Loyalist militia and continued to shoot and stab the defeated enemy combatants before their officers managed to restrain them, claiming revenge for the massacre at Waxhaws.

The destruction of Ferguson's militia, whose commander was killed at King's Mountain, forced Cornwallis to abandon his attempt to invade North Carolina. Meanwhile, Nathanael Greene was on his way south to replace the disgraced Gates as commander of the Southern front. On his way, he stopped off in Philadelphia and pleaded to Congress for more men and supplies, citing the precariousness of the military situation. When Greene arrived at Charlotte, North Carolina, he found 1,400 poorly equipped men who could hardly be called an army waiting for him. In order to transform his army into an effective fighting force, Greene relied on the talents of the Continental Army's best foreign officers. Von Steuben worked tirelessly to train troops in Virginia who could reinforce Greene when required. Kosciuszko and other officers scouted the local terrain to ascertain where the army could fight most effectively.

Greene opted to divide his army into two: the main force headed toward Charleston, while General Daniel Morgan would harass the enemy to the west. Although this was a strategic risk, Greene knew that he could not maintain his entire army by marching down a single route. Morgan's contingent, numbering around 1,000 men, was pursued by Tarleton leading a similar number of men. The two armies met at the Battle of Cowpens in northwestern South Carolina on January 17th, 1781. The battle exemplified Tarleton's recklessness and Morgan's tactical resourcefulness. Morgan's infantry induced Tarleton into launching an assault uphill, and engaged in a melee. After firing a couple of volleys, Morgan's second line retreated and maneuvered around the British left. Meanwhile, the reserve cavalry commanded by Colonel William Washington, a cousin of the commander-in-chief, swept down the hill against the British right flank. With his army surrounded on all sides and facing a bayonet charge from the enemy, Tarleton was forced to surrender, affording a crucial victory to the Continentals.

Once Cornwallis learned of Tarleton's defeat at Cowpens, he sought to hunt down Morgan's contingent. Both Morgan and Greene realized that the former's army presented a vulnerable target for Cornwallis and sought to reunite their forces. Meanwhile, Cornwallis' army was encumbered by a lack of intelligence of the enemy's movements, and failed in his effort to cut off Morgan. The reunited Continental troops opted to retreat and managed to cross into Virginia before the British abandoned the pursuit. Cornwallis established headquarters at Hillsboro, North Carolina and issued a proclamation to loyal Americans to join the fight against the Patriots. Motivated by false reports that Cornwallis' proclamation had been a great success, after receiving reinforcements from von Steuben, Greene led his army back into the Carolinas and awaited a British attack on Guilford Court House. The British scored a tactical victory in the ensuing battle but at the cost of a third of their army, while Greene's men had fought well and remained in high spirits. With 1,400 fit men, Cornwallis made the fateful decision to move north into Virginia in an effort to coordinate with Clinton's army in New York. Meanwhile, Greene led his army south to recapture South Carolina and Georgia. Although Greene lost engagements at Hobkirk's Hill and Eutaw Springs, by September the Patriot militia managed to secure most of the Carolinas and Georgia, leaving the British confined to Charleston and Savannah. Over the course of 1781, the war in the South had turned dramatically in the Americans' favor. The widespread loyalist support envisaged by Cornwallis failed to materialize, and any Loyalist militia who operated in conjunction with the British army were confronted by Patriot militia.

Chapter 10 – Surrender at Yorktown

When Cornwallis arrived in Virginia, he was greeted by Benedict Arnold, who had defected to the British army in late 1780. One of the most talented generals in the Continental Army, Arnold had been given command of the garrison in Philadelphia in 1778. Despite his talent on the battlefield, Arnold's relations with his fellow commanders was poor—his insubordination at Saratoga serving as a prime example—and he was aggrieved that he had been passed for more senior commands. Arnold maintained a lavish lifestyle in Philadelphia and was heavily in debt to London creditors. He had also married the young Peggy Shippen, the daughter of a prominent Loyalist family who had supported the British occupation of Philadelphia. Arnold engaged in secret communications with British commander-in-chief Sir Henry Clinton to surrender the fort of West Point in New York, which he had been appointed to command in April 1779. Through Major John André, the head of espionage for the British forces in North America, Arnold agreed on a payment of £20,000 to surrender the fort. Once he established himself at the fort, he took measures to weaken its defenses. After the two men met in late September, André was captured by American militiamen, and the incriminating letters he carried were sent on to Washington. Once he found out evidence of his treason was sent to Washington, Arnold sailed to New York and received a commission as a British officer. West Point remained in American hands while André was executed by hanging on October 2nd.

In December 1780, Clinton dispatched Arnold to Virginia at the head of the American Legion, a force of 1,600 men, most of whom were deserters from the Continental Army. Arnold managed to capture Richmond by surprise, and continued on a devastating rampage through much of the state, destroying houses and farms in the process. He was forced to relinquish Richmond after the arrival of Lafayette. By March, Arnold received reinforcements commanded by William Phillips, who continued the raiding. Phillips died of fever in May, allowing Arnold to reassume command of the 5,000-man army until Cornwallis' arrival on May 20th. Cornwallis took command from Arnold and sent the latter back to New York. Arnold would spend the rest of the war raiding towns in his native Connecticut. Meanwhile, Cornwallis' army defeated Lafayette and recaptured Richmond. He sent Tarleton on a raid against Charlottesville, where Virginia's legislature had been meeting temporarily. Tarleton narrowly failed to capture Thomas Jefferson, who was serving as governor of Virginia. Jefferson escaped barely ten minutes before the arrival of Tarleton at his home in Monticello, and the British officer contented himself by taking several bottles of wine from Jefferson's cellar.

Cornwallis' decision to march to Virginia was taken without the knowledge of General Clinton at headquarters in New York. Once news of Cornwallis' movements reached Clinton, the British commander-in-chief was obliged to reassess the strategic situation. The southern campaign had been a failure, and expected Loyalist support failed to materialize. British anxieties were heightened by the appearance of a French fleet of twenty ships commanded by

Admiral Paul de Grasse which sailed from Brest in March and arrived in the West Indies at the end of April. Clinton anticipated a Franco-American attack on New York and requested troops from Cornwallis to bolster the defense of New York. The remainder of Cornwallis' forces were authorized to carry out raids on American positions. Clinton also asked Cornwallis to identify a site to establish a deep-water naval port, since the Royal Navy found it difficult to operate from New York. Cornwallis initially demonstrated a reluctance to remain in Virginia and requested permission to return to Charleston, but eventually fulfilled Clinton's orders by moving to Yorktown, located on the southern bank of the York River which flows into the Chesapeake Bay. The new base would allow the British to conduct amphibious operations in Virginia, although Cornwallis was concerned that the Chesapeake's network of rivers would be vulnerable to sudden French attack. Cornwallis decided to keep his entire force of 8,000 men with him to fortify the position, and Clinton approved his dispositions. Cornwallis' army in Virginia was shadowed by Lafayette, who commanded an army half the size.

Clinton's anxieties about a joint Franco-American attack on New York were not misguided. Since July 1780, a French force of 5,000 men sent by King Louis XVI had established itself in Newport, Rhode Island. The army was commanded by the Comte de Rochambeau, an experienced officer in European warfare who could not speak English and had no experience of America. Nevertheless, Rochambeau's military abilities and his readiness to subordinate himself to Washington, were appreciated by the American commander. Although the French had made their landing, Rochambeau was reluctant to leave behind his fleet, which was blockaded by the British Navy. In May 1781, Washington and Rochambeau nevertheless agreed to pursue joint operations against New York City, though these plans did not bear much fruit when put into action in July. In August, Washington received news that de Grasse was sailing to the Chesapeake with 29 ships and over 3,000 men, having made an agreement with the Spanish for the Spanish

Navy to protect French interests in the Caribbean. Washington immediately informed Rochambeau of his intention to lead the two armies to the Chesapeake as quickly as possible. The march exemplified Washington's genius for organization and logistics, and the army arrived in mid-September.

De Grasse arrived in Virginia at the end of August, and at the beginning of September, he fought the British fleet to a standstill in the Battle of the Chesapeake. De Grasse was reluctant to maintain his fleet in the vulnerable waters of the Chesapeake and was hoping to return to the open seas. Washington and Rochambeau persuaded the admiral to stay for the sake of the Franco-American army, and de Grasse agreed to send 2,000 men to assist an allied siege of Yorktown. At the beginning of September, Cornwallis could have attempted to break out of Yorktown against Lafayette's weak force, but stayed put, expecting reinforcements from Clinton. Once the allied army arrived, Cornwallis' chances to fight his way out were slim. Siege operations began on September 28th as the allied army marched from Williamsburg, setting up camp outside Yorktown by the afternoon. Cornwallis established two lines of defense but soon abandoned the outer line. The combined allied army of 19,000 men seemed destined for victory. At times, the allied army silenced their fire and resorted to beating their drums as a show of force against the defenders. Rochambeau soon put an end to this practice, observing that the drumming attracted enemy fire. During the first week of October, allied engineers strengthened their fortifications and constructed positions to station their artillery. The allies began the bombardment on October 9th, their accuracy of fire taking the besieged British army by surprise.

Cornwallis knew that the fall of Yorktown was inevitable. During the night of October 16th, Cornwallis hoped to evacuate his army across the York River to Gloucester Point on the north bank, but poor weather forced him to abandon the attempt. On October 17th, the British fleet sailed from New York with 6,000 reinforcements, but turned back once it realized it was outnumbered by the French fleet. On the same day, without any knowledge of the attempt to aid his besieged army, Cornwallis sent an officer to Washington to negotiate a surrender. Terms were agreed over the following days, and Washington signed on October 19th. The British garrison laid down their arms and marched out of Yorktown playing the British military tune "The World Turned Upside Down," which seemed to perfectly encapsulate the British experience of the war in America. Cornwallis did not attend the surrender ceremony and sent General Charles O'Hara to deliver his sword in his place. Hoping to avoid the humiliation of surrendering to an American officer, O'Hara first sought to deliver the sword to a French officer. The French refused to receive the surrender, and O'Hara was directed to General Benjamin Lincoln, Washington's second-in-command, at Yorktown. Lincoln took the sword and held it briefly before returning it to O'Hara as convention dictated.

The surrender of Cornwallis' army at Yorktown was a major defeat for the British, but did not necessarily signal British defeat in the war. The British continued to possess a large army in New York, and the British army continued to maintain a presence in Charleston, parts of Georgia, Canada, and the West Indies. However, the disaster at Yorktown finally broke the will of the British authorities in London. Lord North, the architect of the policy which led to the war, resigned from the office of prime minister in March 1782. He was replaced by Rockingham, who once again assumed the supreme office. Rockingham's ministry was given the task of negotiating peace with the Americans. Lord Shelburne became Home Secretary (formerly Southern Secretary) with responsibility for colonial affairs, while Charles James Fox was appointed to serve as Foreign Secretary (formerly Northern Secretary) with responsibility for European affairs. Fox and Shelburne were rivals, but under this arrangement they shared responsibility for diplomatic affairs concerning peace between France and America. Shelburne would later become prime minister himself upon Rockingham's death in July. In April, he appointed Richard Oswald, a Scottish merchant who had spent his youth in Virginia, to serve as the British agent in the negotiations. The American Congress appointed John Adams, Benjamin Franklin, and John Jay to serve as peace commissioners, while the peace talks were held in Paris and hosted by French foreign minister Vergennes.

Although Congress instructed the American negotiators to consult with their French allies and follow their advice while conducting talks with the British, American and French interests diverged on the question of the territorial settlement in North America and the commercial rights of the United States in Canada. The French, although recognizing American independence, cared little for such matters and were keen to protect their interests in the Caribbean. Meanwhile, Spain was primarily concerned about recovering Gibraltar, launching a major last-ditch attack on the British outpost in September 1782. The Americans realized they could get better terms by negotiating directly with London. Talks between the British and American representatives were encumbered by the fact that Oswald had not been given instructions to recognize American independence. Franklin and Jay insisted that the British should recognize American independence before the signing of the peace treaty. A new set of words was drafted which managed to satisfy both sides. Preliminary peace articles were finally agreed on November 30th, and Franklin informed Vergennes of the agreement, which would not come into force until the British and French made their peace. The first article of the treaty was an acknowledgment from the British king that the United States were to be "free and sovereign independent states," while the rest of the document delineated the geographical boundaries and commercial rights of this newly recognized sovereign entity. The terms were highly favorable to the Americans, and Shelburne envisaged that the British and Americans could enjoy profitable trade with each other. Congress also agreed to recommend to state legislatures to restore the property rights of British subjects. Despite this undertaking, the states were reluctant to do so, and many Loyalists opted for British exile. The exiles included Benedict Arnold, who had gone to London in a vain attempt to persuade Parliament to continue the war effort.

On January 20th, 1783, peace was signed between Britain and France. French interests in the Caribbean experienced a setback when de Grasse's fleet was defeated by Admiral George Rodney at the Battle of the Saints in April 1782, with its commander falling into British captivity. The French were keen to put an end to a costly war which was draining the royal treasury. Likewise, after their failed attack on Gibraltar, the Spanish also agreed to peace with Britain. They failed to accomplish their primary objective of recapturing Gibraltar, although the British ceded Menorca and the Floridas to the Spanish. All parties signed the Treaty of Paris on September 3rd, 1783, which was ratified the following May. The British army was evacuated from the United States by Guy Carleton, who replaced Clinton in March 1782 and was given the unenviable task of organizing the transport of men and supplies back to Britain. Meanwhile, the victorious Americans celebrated their victory by toasting General Washington, the Continental Army, and their French allies. The bold new experiment to establish a nation dedicated to life, liberty, and the pursuit of happiness had survived a long and agonizing trial by fire. The United States would now have to learn how to govern itself in times of peace.

Chapter 11 – An Imperfect Union

On December 19th, 1783, George Washington rode to Annapolis, Maryland, the temporary seat of Congress. The victorious American commander was the most famous man in North America and the hero of the revolution. Had he desired to do so, Washington could have become a military dictator with the support of the army, as well as most of the people. Instead, having secured the independence of his country with men under arms, Washington relinquished the commission he had been handed by Congress eight years earlier. He was inspired by the example of the Roman general Cincinnatus, who was appointed dictator in 458 BCE and granted exceptional powers to organize the successful defense of the city against an enemy invasion. Once he secured victory within fifteen days, Cincinnatus relinquished his office and returned to his farm. Washington's gesture was also partly motivated by the Newburgh Conspiracy in March 1783. Throughout the war, the Continental Army received limited assistance from Congress, which was unable to compel the states to provide supplies and money to maintain the army. While encamped in Newburgh, New York, army officers who complained that they had not been paid for several months planned a military coup, encouraged by members of Congress who believed that the remit of Congress should be widened at the expense of the states. When Washington uncovered the conspiracy, he quickly moved to defuse the situation, but the risk of the military subverting the civilian government was clear for everyone to see. Congress eventually agreed to keep the men on half-pay for five years, and most of the army was discharged.

The civilian government of the United States operated under the Articles of Confederation, which came into force on March 1st, 1781 following its ratification by all thirteen states. The chief author John Dickinson had recommended granting extensive powers to Congress, but the text that was eventually passed and ratified limited the power of Congress and left most political power in the hands of the states. Congress itself did not have a permanent seat and moved around the union. The initial sessions were based in the Pennsylvania State House in Philadelphia, where the Continental Congress had met and where the Declaration of Independence was signed. The body later moved to Princeton, New Jersey; Annapolis, Maryland; Trenton, New Jersey; and New York City, New York. During the war, individual states understood the imperative of contributing to the war effort and were more willing to act on the recommendations of Congress. Once the Treaty of Paris had been signed, individual states were keen to retain their liberties. Over the course of the 1780s, Congress was faced with a number of challenges in the fields of economics, foreign affairs, and settlement of new territories. These problems required federal solutions and thus the attention of Congress, but owing to the limited powers accorded to Congress under the Articles of Confederation, it would struggle to persuade the states to implement congressional policies.

The national government had significant expenditures from a number of sources, including soldiers' pay, costs of serving public debt, and day-to-day operating costs, but Congress had no source of revenue to call on. The power of taxation lay with the states. In April 1783, Congress passed a measure to impose a rate of 5 percent on imports to finance the payment of the public debt. Although eleven states approved of the measure by 1786, Pennsylvania and New York opposed the duty, and the required unanimity for the levy to become law was not met. Despite attempts by Congress to persuade the states to contribute financially, in 1785 Congress stopped paying the interest on its debt to France, and in 1787 it defaulted on part of the principal. The drain on the French treasury due to the war partially contributed to the French Revolution in 1789.

In addition to its concerns about public finance, Congress was also concerned about commercial issues. Although trade volumes increased after the war, there remained a sense of unease about falling prices, heavy indebtedness, and inconsistent trade regulation which restricted interstate trade. In 1786, Congressman James Madison of Virginia suggested a convention of states to consider strengthening the powers of Congress to include the regulation of trade and powers of taxation. Only five states attended the convention, and there was little it could do to persuade the other states to cede their powers to Congress.

While Congress was hoping for state approval of the import tax, the national government had to deal with a foreign policy crisis. Although the British had agreed to a generous territorial settlement with the United States, Spain did not recognize the cession of territory east of the Mississippi to American control. Britain and United States had agreed in Paris that the Mississippi River should be open to merchant vessels from both countries, but in 1784, the Spanish closed the lower Mississippi to American navigation. They hoped to persuade settlers in what would become Kentucky and Tennessee to break away from the United States in order to trade through the Spanish port of New Orleans. These settlers seriously considered this as they felt they were neglected by Congress. The United States secretary of foreign affairs at this time was John Jay, a New York lawyer who had previously served as ambassador to

Spain and as one of the peace negotiators in Paris. Jay's instructions were drafted by Virginian Congressman James Monroe, which defended the American claim to territories east of the Mississippi and claimed the right of navigation along the whole length of the river. However, as an Easterner, Jay was keen to avoid competition from western states trading via the Mississippi, and was open to accepting Spanish demands. He requested the authority from Congress to provide him with new instructions, but these were not granted as any treaty required the support of nine states for approval. The disputes over Jay's actions hindered further cooperation between the states.

Congress was more successful in regulating the settlement and government of territories to the northwest of the Ohio River. The territory had been claimed by Virginia since the seventeenth century, but it ceded its claim in 1781 as a condition of Maryland's ratification of the Articles of Confederation. Thomas Jefferson, who served on the congressional committee overseeing the settlement of new territories, envisaged that after a period of territorial government these new lands would join the union with the same status as the original thirteen states. Jefferson also believed that the new territories should be given to settlers for free, but Congress was short of funds and decided to sell land in order to pay off the national debt. In the Land Ordinance of 1785, Congress divided the new territory into townships of 36 square miles with lots of one square miles on sale for at least one dollar per acre. Provisions were also made for land grants to veteran soldiers and public schools. The scheme soon fell victim to speculation, with the Ohio Company buying up the land at low prices. Squatters who settled in the Ohio territory without any right to the land also complicated matters and often found themselves in conflict with local Indian populations. This anarchic process of settlement forced Congress to revise its policy by introducing the Northwest Ordinance of 1787, which gave Congress control of the government. The ordinance was also the first document in American history to prohibit slavery.

Despite the success in the regulation of western settlement, by the late 1780s, there was a general sense that American society and government had failed to realize the idealistic expectations of freedom and progress that fueled the nation during the war against Britain. Thomas Jefferson believed that the principles of liberty and freedom set out in the Declaration of Independence should be translated to American society. As a member of the Virginia House of Delegates, and later as the state's governor, Jefferson hoped to introduce a state constitution that would recognize these principles. He envisaged that the poorest members of society would be granted land for free to develop and cultivate. He believed that slavery was incompatible with liberty and recognized that the institution should somehow come to an end, and advocated enhanced legal rights for slaves. Nevertheless, Jefferson should not be regarded as a racial egalitarian—he was a slaveowner himself, and recent evidence shows that he kept a slave mistress, Sally Hemmings. Jefferson's preferred option to address slavery was colonization, whereby black slaves would be sent to distant territories to keep them apart from the white American population. Jefferson's vision was largely rejected by the state assembly. The Virginia gentry which controlled state government were keen to maintain the privileges they enjoyed before the revolution. Most Virginians therefore did not encounter much of a change from British rule, with the fabric of society remaining the same. If the United States were to realize its aspirations for freedom and liberty, it had to reduce the power of established state elites who had little to gain and a lot to lose.

The widespread recognition that the Articles of Confederation were not fit for purpose led to calls to amend the document and strengthen the national government. These voices grew louder in the aftermath of Shays' Rebellion in 1786. Daniel Shays was a Massachusetts farmer who had served in the Continental Army at the very beginning of the war at Lexington and Concord. Shays and his supporters, most of whom were farmers from central and western Massachusetts, suffered from the state's financial policy. The state government in Massachusetts was dominated by merchants who imposed high taxes to finance the state debt and its obligations to Congress. These measures eventually provoked a rebellion in August 1786 after the state legislature failed to consider the many petitions for debt relief. Over the ensuing months, the rebellion spread throughout the state, and in January 1787, the rebels threatened to take control of the federal armory at Springfield. Congress was unable to supply an army to suppress the rebellion, so it was up to the authorities at Massachusetts to do so. The state militia, under the command of General William Shepard, seized control of the armory without authorization from Congress, while General Benjamin Lincoln commanded a private militia to confront Shays. By June 1787, the rebellion was successfully suppressed, but it was clear to everyone that radical changes needed to be made if the United States were to survive and fulfill its promise of building a new society.

Chapter 12 – A More Perfect Union

The leading American politicians who recognized that the Articles of Confederation were unsatisfactory met in Philadelphia in May 1787 to discuss proposals to amend the articles. Most of these men, although loyal to their own states, recognized that the authority of the national government had to be increased. James Madison was among the most enthusiastic advocates for increasing the powers of the national government. A member of the Virginia delegation, Madison had been instrumental in convening the Annapolis Convention the previous year, which looked at the question of interstate trade. While there were only five states represented at Annapolis, delegates from twelve states met at Philadelphia—only Rhode Island did not send a delegation. Among Madison's fellow delegates from Virginia was General Washington himself, who had been persuaded to return to politics following his retirement from public life after he relinquished the office of commander-in-chief. Although Washington did not have particularly sophisticated views about how the new government should be structured, his experience with dealing with Congress during the war convinced him that the national government required greater powers. Washington, who continued to enjoy the reputation of a national hero, would also lend further legitimacy to the Philadelphia Convention and any recommendations it would make to the states. Washington was soon elected chairman of the Convention.

The delegates soon decided that the Articles of Confederation could not be amended and a new constitution was required to establish the powers of a new national government. Madison proposed that the government should consist of three separate branches: the legislative, the executive, and the judiciary. The doctrine of separation of powers was inspired by the French philosopher Montesquieu's *The Spirit of the Laws*, which was inspired by the British constitution. The legislature would propose and vote on the laws, the executive would implement them, and the judiciary would ensure that the laws were being followed. While these functions were separated in the British government, they could not be said to be independent. Members of the Houses of Parliament formed both the executive and the judiciary. In the new American constitution, individuals would only serve in one branch of government with very few exceptions. The legislative branch served to ensure that the government would remain accountable to the people. Madison initially proposed that Congress should be bicameral—consisting of two chambers—where the lower house would be directly elected by the people, while the upper house would be chosen by members of the lower house. Proposed legislation would have to meet the approval of both houses before becoming law. The legislative branch would have the power to raise taxation, declare war, and make treaties, the primary functions for any government. The powers of the legislative branch would be laid out in Article I of the new Constitution.

Members of the convention soon split into two camps by the question of state representation in the new legislature. Edmund

Randolph of Virginia presented a plan, largely drafted by Madison, which proposed that states should be represented in Congress according to the size of their population. According to this principle, which became known as the Virginia Plan, the more populous states would enjoy greater representation in the national legislature. Virginia's proposal was supported by Pennsylvania and Massachusetts, the second and third most populous states in the union. The smaller states resisted the proposal, recognizing that their representation would be diminished. The three largest states accounted for almost half the American population and would therefore control half the votes in Congress. The smaller states, such as Delaware, Maryland, and even New York, which remained sparsely populated at this stage, supported the plan put forward by New Jersey's William Paterson. The New Jersey Plan proposed that each state's representation would be equal regardless of its population. This was effectively the same principle which governed the Articles of Confederation, where each state could cast one vote in Congress regardless of its size. Eventually Connecticut delegates Oliver Ellsworth and Roger Sherman proposed that a Congress divided into two houses could have proportional representation in the lower house (the House of Representatives) and equal representation in the upper house (the Senate). Although the Pennsylvania and Virginia delegates continued to oppose this, it was eventually approved by the Convention on July 16th, 1787.

A crucial element of the question of representation related to the way in which slaves should be accounted for in determining the representation of the lower house. Slaves were denied the right to vote and therefore would not be represented in the legislature. However, the Southern states, including South Carolina and Georgia, had large slave populations who worked on plantations. These Southern states recognized the predominantly anti-slavery sentiment in the North, and understood that they would need to fight in Congress to preserve the institution of slavery which sustained their economies. If slaves were not counted toward representation, then the Southern states would have a lesser voice in debates. The Convention eventually used the formula by which each slave would account for three-fifths of a freeman in determining the representation for each state. The same formula had been suggested by Madison in 1783 to determine the financial contribution of each state to Congress. Although many Northerners were uncomfortable with making this compromise, the Convention did so in order to ensure that South Carolina and Georgia would remain part of the union. The debate over slavery extended to the Atlantic slave trade. Although many delegates hoped to abolish the import of slaves across the Atlantic, as a compromise the Convention agreed to abolish the external slave trade only by 1808. The question of slavery was one of the most contentious debates during the Philadelphia Convention, but the delegates were careful not to employ the term "slave" in their deliberations. In the eventual document they were referred to as "all other persons."

The deliberations over representation in Congress gave way to the discussions concerning the executive branch. The head of the executive branch would be the president of the United States of America. By virtue of his office, the president would become the commander-in-chief of the United States' armed forces and given the right to appoint army officers. The president was also given the power to appoint ambassadors and federal judges, pending Senate approval. The president's term limits were extended to four years with the right to reelection, though there were disagreements about how the president should be chosen. Madison believed that the president should be elected by the people, but others believed that this could not guarantee that the president would be an individual who was fit for office. The Convention temporarily agreed on July 17th for the president to be elected by the national legislature, but later opted for an electoral college. The states would appoint a number of electors equal to their entire congressional representation who would cast two votes. The individual who received the largest number of votes would serve as president, and the second highest would be vice president. A tie would be determined by the House of Representatives, with each state casting one vote each. In the event that no candidates were to secure a majority of electoral votes, the House of Representatives would choose the president from the five candidates who secured the most votes. The presidency was therefore indirectly elected, though some states opted to allow the electors to be chosen by the people through elections, while others nominated electors through their state legislatures. The powers of the executive were outlined in Article II of the Constitution signed by the Philadelphia Convention. The powers of the judicial branch were outlined in Article III, providing for a Supreme Court of the United States populated by justices appointed by the president for life. On September 17th, 39 of the 55 men who attended the Convention signed the Constitution.

A Constitution had been signed, but there was no guarantee that the states would ratify the new document. Ratification required the approval of nine states, and as soon the Philadelphia Convention had finished its business, the public debate began about the merits of the proposals it produced. The first articles criticizing the proposed Constitution appeared in the press in late September and early October under the pseudonyms of "Cato" and "Brutus," key figures of the Roman Republic. They argued that the new constitution would override the sovereignty of the individual states and make them vulnerable to the tyranny of the central government. They feared that the president would become an effective monarch. In response to these criticisms of the Constitution which would become known as the *Anti-Federalist Papers*, Alexander Hamilton of New York embarked on a project to persuade the states of the merits of the Constitution. A former artillery officer in the Continental Army who served on Washington's staff and later played a key role at the Battle of Yorktown, Hamilton had been a delegate at the Constitutional Convention, though his contribution to the debates was limited. Hamilton published the first of 85 articles, collectively known to history as the *Federalist Papers*, on October 27th, 1787 under the pseudonym "Publius," in honor of Publius Valerius Poplicola, one of the founders of the Roman Republic. In *Federalist Paper* No. 1, Hamilton explained why the union of the states would serve to encourage national prosperity, highlighting the inadequacy of the Articles of Confederation and how the Constitution could serve to protect liberty, property, and the American republic.

Federalist Paper No. 1 outlined the themes that would be covered in the rest of the *Federalist Papers*. Hamilton initially approached his fellow New Yorker John Jay as a collaborator on this project, and Jay duly produced four powerful pieces to follow up Hamilton's first one. After this, Jay fell ill and would only contribute one more article in the series, No. 64. In light of Jay's illness, Hamilton turned to James Madison. The two men worked at a frantic pace, publishing three or four articles a week for several months. Madison's output consisted of at least 29 articles, many of which addressed the concerns of the Anti-Federalists. In response to the fears of tyrannical government, Hamilton and Madison argued that the union was on the verge of collapse, and any dissolution of the union would result in the states coming into conflict with each other, which would make the American republic vulnerable to the designs of European monarchies. They also proposed that any difference in opinion over economic and political interests should be settled in a representative Congress. Madison believed that a clearly defined system and the Constitution's clear delineation of the powers of the federal government would protect the states' rights and individual liberties. Moreover, Madison discussed measures to prevent the tyranny of the majority, and supported the expansion of the United States into a large commercial republic in *Federalist Paper* No. 10. In *Federalist Paper* Nos. 39 and 51, he espoused the principles behind the separation of powers into three branches, as well as the sharing of power between the federal government and the states. The independent branches of government would provide checks and balances on the other and prevent the tyranny of the majority.

Although the *Federalist Papers* were initially published in New York and addressed "To the State and People of New York," they contributed to the national debate concerning ratification and were used by advocates of the Constitution across the union. In the months following the signing of the Constitution, state conventions met to discuss the issue of ratification. Delaware was the first state to ratify, doing so on December 7th. It was soon joined by Pennsylvania, which was destined to be a lynchpin of the new union, and within a month five states had approved the Constitution. In February 1788, Massachusetts approved the Constitution by a narrow margin, with John Hancock and Samuel Adams being persuaded to support the Federalist cause despite some reservations. By June, following New Hampshire's decision to ratify, the Constitution had the support of the nine states that it required to come into force. But two powerful states, Virginia and New York, remained on the sidelines. After intense debate, Virginia ratified it at the end of June. New York was reluctant to ratify the Constitution without a Bill of Rights protecting the rights of the people and the states. Alexander Hamilton had argued against this in *Federalist Paper* No. 84, arguing that the Constitution did not exist to limit the people's rights, but to define the scope of the federal government. Nevertheless, New York only ratified in July on the condition that a Bill of Rights would be introduced. When the new Congress met in the spring of 1789, it prepared a Bill of Rights which was drafted by Madison. Of the twelve articles presented, ten were ratified by 1791. The First Amendment enshrined the freedom of speech among other freedoms, the Second Amendment protected the right to bear arms to protect against tyranny, while the Tenth Amendment stipulated that all powers which were not delegated to the national government were reserved to the states and the people. North Carolina and Rhode Island finally ratified the Constitution in November 1789 and June 1790 respectively and subsequently joined the union.

Chapter 13 – Manifest Destiny

The United States Constitution proved to be a remarkably enduring document. Since the passage of the Bill of Rights, it has been amended only on seventeen further occasions. This was far from guaranteed when the Constitution came into force in July 1788. The federal government began its operations on March 4th, 1789. On that day, members of Congress opened the new congressional session in New York. On April 6th, Congress met to certify the results of the first presidential election. George Washington had been elected unanimously to the presidency. John Adams, who received the second highest number of votes, became vice president. Washington was notified of the results on April 14th and inaugurated at Federal Hall in New York on April 30th. In September, Washington appointed John Jay to serve as the first chief justice of the Supreme Court and chose five other associate justices. The three branches of the federal government were thus in place.

In the summer of 1789, Congress would create three executive departments to assist Washington in the management of government affairs: the state department with responsibility for foreign affairs, the war department for military affairs, and the treasury with responsibility for public finances. Washington appointed Thomas Jefferson as secretary of state. Henry Knox and Alexander Hamilton, two of Washington's former staff officers, were appointed to serve as secretary of war and secretary of the treasury respectively. As a leading advocate for the federal government, Hamilton was the driving force of Washington's administration. Hamilton pursued an agenda to transform the United States into an economic and commercial powerhouse by establishing a system of national credit supported by the First Bank of the United States. While Washington favored Hamilton's stance and approved many of his treasury secretary's proposals, he was keen to appease Jefferson, who was an opponent of Hamilton's attempts to create new federal institutions. Jefferson was concerned that the measures to encourage commerce would favor the Northern states at the expense of the Southern states. As a compromise, in 1790 Hamilton agreed to support proposals to relocate the national capital farther south near Georgetown on the Potomac River. The territory was named District of Columbia and the city named Washington after the president. The federal government temporarily moved to Philadelphia and building work on the new capital began in 1791. Washington had planned to retire from the presidency after a single term, but was persuaded to stay in office for a second term from 1793 to 1797. In 1796, at the end of his second term, Washington decided to relinquish his office, setting a precedent that would not be broken until the 1940s. In his farewell address, published in September 1796, Washington warned the American political classes from engaging in factionalism, which would be injurious to the cause of liberty. Washington's warning fell on deaf ears. The disputes between Hamilton and Jefferson provided the context for the first party system, pitting Hamilton's Federalists against Jeffersonian Republicans. Following Washington's retirement in 1797, John Adams was elected president while Jefferson became vice president. Adams was a Federalist and continued to pursue Hamilton's policies in office. This arrangement meant that the president and vice president were members of opposing parties, and soon the two men, erstwhile friends and leaders of the revolution, were no longer on speaking terms. The first party system would continue until the late 1810s with the Jeffersonian Republicans becoming dominant after the Federalists were considered sympathetic to British interests during the War of 1812 against the British. However, although the fortunes of the parties in question would rise and fall, American politics continue to be dominated by two major parties to the present day.

The uncomfortable situation of president and vice president representing different parties was addressed in the 1800 election when the leading candidates for president selected a running mate as vice president. In order to ensure that the candidates from the same party would not be tied, it was expected that one of the electors would cast a vote for the presidential candidate, and his second vote for a third individual. The Jeffersonians narrowly won the election, with Jefferson winning 73 votes to Adams' 65. However, in the reckoning of the final results, Jefferson and his running mate Aaron Burr both received 73 electoral votes. The tied election was thus thrown to the outgoing House of Representatives, which was controlled by the Federalists. The Federalists saw Jefferson as their leading opponent and sought to deprive him of the presidency by favoring Burr. Hamilton, who no longer held public office, recognized that his fellow New Yorker Burr was the greater threat to the Federalist cause and sought to persuade the Federalist congressmen to support Jefferson. Jefferson was duly elected to the presidency on the 36th ballot in the House vote, with Burr as vice president. Hamilton's intervention to deny Burr the presidency would have long-lasting repercussions. In July 1804, the two men fought a duel, motivated by the 1800 election as well as local New York politics. Hamilton was mortally wounded by Burr, whose political career ended as a result. In order to prevent a recurrence of the crisis of 1800, the 12th Amendment was passed to establish separate elections in the electoral college for president and vice president.

By the early 1800s, the political institutions and processes that would define the United States government had largely been established. Its territorial extent, however, was a fraction of its present size, though new states were already being admitted into the union. The Treaty of Paris had established the western borders of the United States at the Mississippi, though this was disputed by Spain. In 1800, Spain returned the Louisiana Territory to France in exchange for territories in Italy conquered by the French revolutionary armies. Napoleon Bonaparte, who had recently come to power in a military coup, sought to re-establish French commercial interests in North America. The American settlers in the west were concerned about French ambitions in Louisiana, and in 1803, Jefferson's government approached Napoleon, offering to purchase the port of New Orleans from France for $10 million, to ensure that US merchants could trade freely along the whole length of the Mississippi River. Napoleon responded positively to this approach since the French government was in the process of preparing for the resumption of hostilities in Britain. The defeat of the French in the Haitian Revolution of 1803 had presented a setback for Napoleon's North American project. The French therefore offered to sell the whole of Louisiana for $15 million, an offer which was immediately accepted by American agents. The French hoped that American possession of Louisiana would encourage the United States to become a commercial power and a counterweight to British interests.

In 1804, Jefferson sent an expedition of US Army volunteers under the command of Meriwether Lewis and William Clark to survey the new territories he had purchased. The Lewis and Clark expedition set off from St. Louis in May 1804 and traversed the entire Louisiana Territory, encountering many Indian tribes in the process. They then moved farther west through land claimed by the British until they reached the Pacific in November 1805. The expedition team made their return journey the following spring and arrived back in St. Louis in September 1806. Lewis and Clark reported back extensive scientific, geographical, and ethnographical information about the Louisiana Territory, and the expedition also served to lay claim to the Pacific territories. Over the following decades, waves of American settlers would flock westwards in an effort to seek their fortune and escape economic hardship. As increasing numbers of Americans settled these new lands, they came into conflict with indigenous peoples. In the 1800s, five Indian nations in the southeast had been guaranteed the status of autonomous nations by the United States in an effort to encourage their assimilation to American culture, but pressures of American settlement led to land disputes. In 1830, President Andrew Jackson signed the Indian Removal Act which forced the five tribes to relinquish their lands in exchange for less fertile lands to the west in what would become Oklahoma Territory. The measure was violently resisted, and thousands of Indians died as they were forcibly removed on the so-called Trail of Tears during the 1830s.

The purchase of Louisiana more than doubled the size of the United States, but there were still extensive territories to the west controlled by the Spanish Empire. In 1821, these territories became part of Mexico after the latter gained independence from their European colonial masters. American settlers established themselves in the Mexican state of Texas over the 1820s, and soon hostilities broke out against the Mexicans, resulting in Texan independence from Mexico in 1836. The Republic of Texas would later be admitted to the United States in 1846 during the presidency of James K. Polk. Polk believed that it was the manifest destiny of the United States to extend its republican principles across the continent and laid claim to further Mexican territory to the southwest, as well as British lands to the northwest. The Mexican-American War (1846-48) proved to be a catastrophic defeat for the Mexicans. In the ensuing Treaty of Guadalupe Hidalgo, Mexico ceded half its lands to the United States. Polk also brokered a settlement with the British which provided for

American control of the southern half of Oregon Country, which would become the states of Washington and Oregon. With these territorial acquisitions, the United States expanded to the Pacific Coast and assumed much of its current territorial extent.

The westward expansion of the United States did not only lead to clashes with Indians, but further fueled the debate over the future of slavery. The United States had been established on a contradictory basis of recognizing the liberties of all men while holding black slaves in bondage. The union was balanced between the Northern anti-slavery states and the Southern slave-owning states. Although the Northern states believed that the federal government did not have the constitutional power to abolish slavery where it already existed, they opposed the further expansion of slavery. With the admission of each new state into the union, each with two senators, this threatened to alter the political balance between the Northern and Southern states. The debate over the admission of Missouri in 1820 threatened the future of the union. Eventually a compromise was brokered by Henry Clay of Kentucky, whereby Missouri would be admitted as a slave state but it would be balanced out by the admission of Maine, formerly part of Massachusetts, as a free state. Territories north of Missouri's southern border would henceforth be restricted to slavery, while those south of the line were open to slavery. This was the first of a set of uneasy compromises over the first half of the nineteenth century. The incorporation of California into the union following the Mexican War resulted in a further compromise over slavery in 1850, once again brokered by Clay at the age of 73.

The disputes over the expansion of slavery continued into the 1850s over the admission of Kansas and Nebraska into the union. The admission of these states was a precondition for the construction of a transcontinental railroad linking Chicago to the Pacific, championed by Senator Stephen Douglas of Illinois. Although both territories were north of the Missouri Compromise Line, Southern senators refused to vote for admission unless slavery was permitted. Douglas suggested that the extension of slavery should depend on the principle of popular sovereignty, allowing the territories themselves to vote on the question. This principle was part of the Kansas-Nebraska Act of 1854, which repealed the Missouri Compromise. The popular sovereignty clause resulted in pro- and anti-slavery factions traveling to Kansas to vote on the issue of slavery, resulting in bloody clashes between the two sides. The violence in Kansas foreshadowed the US Civil War (1861-65), a conflict fundamentally caused by disagreements over slavery. The victory of the US federal government against the Confederate States of America resulted in the abolition of slavery, firstly with the Emancipation Proclamation issued by President Abraham Lincoln in 1863, and officially with the Thirteenth Amendment in 1865. With the abolition of slavery, one of the fundamental contradictions of the American revolutionary years was seemingly resolved.

Conclusion

The success of the American Revolution could be seen as a miracle, by which a colonial militia of farmers and merchants managed to defeat the most professional army in the world. On the other hand, the British defeat could also be seen as an inevitable consequence of attempts to fight a war across an ocean in hostile territory against a people fighting not only for their homes and families, but for a new form of society. Despite the disputes between the states and the relative weakness of the central government, and the often desperate situation of the Continental Army, the Americans avoided defeat in large part due to their commitment to the cause of liberty. Nevertheless, American victory cannot be explained purely in terms of the actions taken by Congress or by Washington and his army. Without French assistance, the war could have been dragged out for much longer. The fact that the war ended when it did, following Cornwallis' defeat at the Siege of Yorktown, was largely the consequence of the changing political environment in London.

British policy transformed from attempting to suppress the revolution to encouraging the development of the United States as a close commercial partner.

Compared to the monarchical societies in Europe, the new American republic seemed to represent democratic progress. American political leaders established their state under the inspiration of the liberal political philosophy of Montesquieu and John Locke, and the iconography of Republican Rome. However, as in Rome, the right to life, liberty, and the pursuit of happiness was largely restricted to white men. The rights of the indigenous population were largely ignored as American settlement extended farther west, despite the assistance many Indian peoples provided to the new settlers. Slavery remained legal and constitutional in the United States for ninety years after independence, and necessitated a devastating civil war before the institution was abolished. Even after the abolition of slavery, African-Americans found it difficult to achieve racial equality. The racial prejudices of white Americans continued to define Southern society. African-Americans were barred from voting through intimidation and quasi-discriminatory laws, such as literacy tests. It took until the 1960s, a century after the abolition of slavery, for the civil rights movement to secure greater protections for African-Americans in the United States. It was a similar tale for women, who were only granted the right to vote in 1920 after a century of protest. The election of Barack Obama to the US presidency in 2008 was a major sign of progress, but racial and gender discrimination remains prevalent in American society.

For all its faults, the history of the United States is a tale of progress and success. From a loose confederation of thirteen colonies in the 18th century, in less than two hundred years it had become the most powerful nation in the world. Some of the reasons for American success can be found in the rights enshrined in the Declaration of Independence and the US Constitution. The United States advertised itself as a land of opportunity for Europeans seeking better livelihoods. Andrew Carnegie immigrated to the United States from

Scotland as a child in 1848, and built a railroad and steel business empire which made him one of the wealthiest men in the world and a famous philanthropist. Albert Einstein found his home in the United States after Adolf Hitler came to power in his native Germany in 1933. Another Jewish émigré, Henry Kissinger, would become one of the country's most influential statesmen in the 1970s and 80s, a political giant of the age. The ability of the United States to attract talent from all over the world, its spirit of liberalism and constitutional rule in politics and economics, and the idea of American exceptionalism have all contributed to the United States becoming the most powerful nation in the world. American corporations from Microsoft and Apple to McDonalds and Coca-Cola have left their mark throughout the globe.

Although the United States has changed much over the last two and a half centuries, the debates that dominate American political discourse today strongly reflect the same debates during the American Revolution and the early days of the American republic. Issues such as rights and freedoms, the balance of power between federal and state government, and the need to protect liberty in the face of tyranny have been a part of American political discourse since the Massachusetts rebels threw the tea into Boston Harbor. The Founding Fathers of the United States did not share a single political philosophy, and many were initially reluctant to support calls for independence. The United States won its independence through George Washington's army and Thomas Paine's writings, and the early republic was forged through the dynamic tension between the followers of Hamilton and Jefferson, each of whom shaped the United States in their own manner. All of these men believed fundamentally in the rights and liberties of the American people, but had different conceptions about their extent and how best to protect them from tyranny. In order to understand the United States today, it is worth understanding the principles which inspired the founding of the United States, and the circumstances under which it secured its independence.

Here are some other Captivating History books that you might be interested in

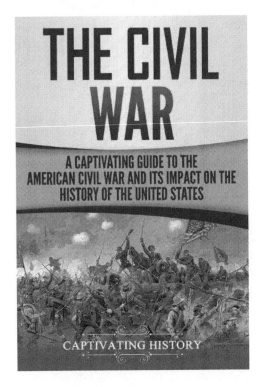

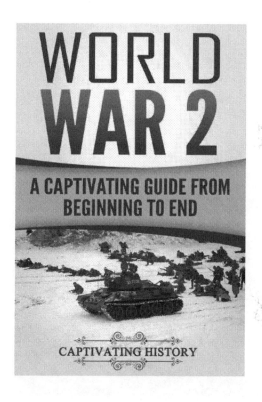

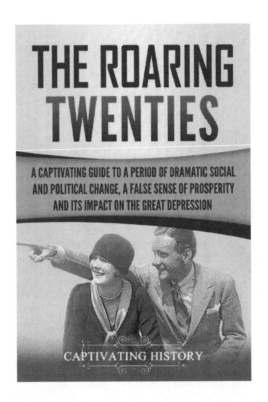

THE ROARING
TWENTIES

A CAPTIVATING GUIDE TO A PERIOD OF DRAMATIC SOCIAL
AND POLITICAL CHANGE, A FALSE SENSE OF PROSPERITY
AND ITS IMPACT ON THE GREAT DEPRESSION

CAPTIVATING HISTORY

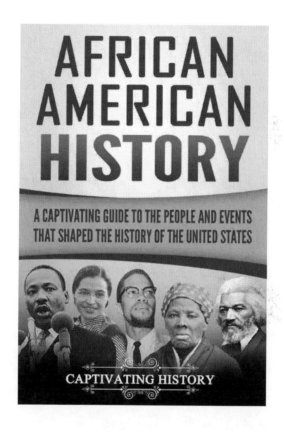

Free Bonus from Captivating History (Available for a Limited time)

Hi History Lovers!

Now you have a chance to join our exclusive history list so you can get your first history ebook for free as well as discounts and a potential to get more history books for free! Simply visit the link below to join.

Captivatinghistory.com/ebook

Also, make sure to follow us on:

Twitter: @Captivhistory

Facebook: Captivating History:@captivatinghistory

Further Reading

Brogan, H., *The Penguin History of the United States* (London, 1990).

Chernow, R., *Alexander Hamilton* (New York, 2004).

Chernow, R., *Washington: A Life* (New York, 2010).

Ferling, J., *Almost A Miracle: The American Victory in the War of Independence* (Oxford, 2009).

McCullough, D., *1776: America and Britain at War* (New York, 2005).

Meacham, J., *Thomas Jefferson: The Art of Power* (New York, 2012).

Middlekauff, R., *The Glorious Cause: The American Revolution, 1763-1789* (Oxford, 2005).

Reynolds, D., *America: Empire of Liberty* (London, 2010).

Taylor, A., *American Revolutions: A Continental History, 1750-1804* (New York, 2016).

Van Cleve, G., *We Have Not a Government: The Articles of Confederation and the Road to the Constitution* (Chicago, 2017).

Wood, G. S., *The American Revolution: A History* (New York, 2003).